Mark's Gospel, the Whole Story

Bible Study for Ordinary Readers

BY JOAN MITCHELL, CSJ

Good Ground Press

Sisters of St. Joseph of Carondelet,
1884 Randolph Avenue   St. Paul, MN 55105
1-800-232-5533 goodgroundpress.com

Christians today live in the resonance
of the word that Jesus taught,
the eyewitness disciples proclaimed,
the first Christian communities shaped
and Mark was the first to write down.
The story echoes down the centuries,
comes to voice again at worship,
and embodiment in all who live its message.

Book and Cover Design: Jennifer Poferl

ISBN: 1-885996-52-7

CONTENTS

It's a Story

Through the centuries the Church, its ministers and scholars, have put Mark in fourth place among the four gospels—the least significant, the white ribbon. Mark gets credit for collecting and writing down the gospel narrative for the first time but little praise for artistry. Both Matthew and Luke use the narrative Mark constructs but edit, rearrange, and draw in additional traditions to convey their own insights into Jesus' identity, ministry, and message.

Matthew gets the blue ribbon for most attention to Church interests and longest sermon (the sayings that comprise the Sermon on the Mount, chapters 5-7). Luke gets a grand champion purple for literary elegance and theological insight, hanging Jesus' identity on Isaiah's promises of a Spirit-filled prophet who brings good news to the poor and like Israel in exile has to suffer. John's gospel takes the prize in a whole different category with its theology of Jesus as the preexistent Word and its own distinct composition around seven revealing signs.

Uniquely Mark's gospel preserves the way early communities told and shaped Jesus' story in their oral traditions. These early communities gathered around the eyewitness disciples to remember Jesus' teachings and actions and break bread as he asked. Jesus himself never wrote a word. He taught and preached orally. No one captured on their smart phone a video of Jesus teaching or healing. No hidden security camera preserved his activities. It is the men and women disciples who accompany Jesus in his ministry that remember and hand on his teachings and actions and proclaim them in the light of his resurrection.

The Acts of the Apostles, the sequel to Luke's gospel, tells us the tongues of Jesus' disciples caught fire on Pentecost, and they began proclaiming their Easter experience that God raised up Jesus, who was crucified. Early believers formed communities and house churches in which they broke bread as Jesus asked and became workshops of the word, gathering to hear about Jesus' words and deeds from those who accompanied him. Story hearers became storytellers.

WHAT ABOUT ORAL TRADITION?

Oral storytelling gives events plot, character, and form just as written stories do. Mark's gospel richly exhibits oral artistry and theological insights. Oral traditions differ from the game of telephone, which results often in silly, indecipherable messages. Oral sayings and stories have bones, basic structures that aid memory and fix essential messages. For example, its inverse form makes the saying, "The Sabbath is made for humankind, not humankind for the

Sabbath," easy to remember. The passion narrative fixes places and scenes indelibly in Christian memory—supper in the upper room, prayer in the garden, trial at the high priest's house, mocking and scourging at the soldiers' fortress, condemnation at Pilate's quarters, crucifixion at Golgotha.

The gospel we receive not only conveys Jesus' message but proclaims the first Christians' faith that his resurrection affirms Jesus is the messiah and God's Son. Their faith colors the whole story. The gospel contains three layers of history and insight. It narrates events and teachings from Jesus' public ministry (A.D. 30). It hands on stories and sayings early Christian communities told and shaped orally during the four decades between Jesus' death and resurrection and Mark writing the first gospel (A.D. 30-70). The evangelist Mark preserves the traditions by writing them down at a time when the eyewitnesses are dying out and the siege of Jerusalem has scattered the original community (A.D. 70).

In the written gospel an all-knowing or omniscient narrator takes the place of the oral preacher or storyteller. As the narrative engages us, we forget that anyone is telling the story; its plot and scenes unfold as if they were happening. But many eyewitnesses and early Christians have told and shaped the traditions we receive, and the gospel writer has arranged them purposely to reflect theologically on who Jesus is. Like the early believers we have well-developed storytelling and story-interpreting skills ourselves from hearing jokes, watching soap operas, or prefering the pattern of one murder series or comedy series over another. Once we realize that the early Christian witnesses give stories forms that stick in the memory and arrange stories deliberately, we can use our skills to interpret their claims and insights.

The gospel refers back in history to events in Jesus' life, the world behind the text. In the gospel Jesus' teachings and actions take literary form and become story—the world of the text. The gospel also refers forward to its audiences—the world ahead of the text. Mark writes this gospel for us—for future hearers and readers. We are the ones meant to catch on to the whole story that Jesus' disciples in their pre-Easter character don't get. In written form the gospel travels through time and space, calling new generations to faith in "the good news of Jesus Christ, the Son of God" (1.1).

WHEN WAS THE FIRST GOSPEL WRITTEN?

Scholars date the writing of Mark's gospel about A.D. 70 when the Romans destroyed the temple in Jerusalem and ended temple-centered religious practice. In the decade before the destruction of the temple, officials martyred in Rome two of the early Christians' strongest preachers and leaders—Peter and Paul, silencing their voices. In the same years the disciples who knew Jesus firsthand were growing old. Anyone who was 30 in A.D. 30 during Jesus' ministry is 70 at the time of the writing of the first gospel. If Jairus's daughter, who was 12 when Jesus raised her from death, remains alive in A.D. 70, she is 52, and can tell the story of what happened to her. In A.D. 70 the era of eyewitnesses handing on their stories is ending. For the gospel to continue to call new generations to faith, it must be written down so the message can travel through time.

Mark's gospel is the product of crisis. The other three gospel writers may convey fuller accounts of Jesus' life, death, and resurrection, but Mark's gospel brings us closest to the generation that faced the end of the eyewitness era and temple-centered Judaism and lived faithfully into the future without knowing Jesus' message would last and transform the world. Some scholars connect the gospel writer Mark with John Mark, who accompanied Paul (Acts 12.12,25; 13.5,13). Tradition identifies Peter as his source and Christians in Rome as the community for whom he writes after the martyrdoms of Peter and Paul in the A.D. 60s. Other scholars place Mark and his audience in Israel in the aftermath of the destruction of Jerusalem and the temple in A.D. 70. In either case the gospel responds to a crisis; its audience fears the future. The gospel calls this audience and us beyond fear for their lives to faith in Jesus.

BECOMING ACTIVE READERS

As a whole literary work, the gospel requires active readers to find the insights early Christians oral traditions stash in the narrative for us readers of the future. As the first written gospel, Mark preserves not just individual stories but whole sequences of oral storytelling. These sequences are not just bites of tradition but sandwiches and whole meals on a skewer; they are story strands already arranged into patterns that proclaim Jesus' message and believers' insights. Repeatedly Mark creates literary sandwiches by placing one story within another. For example, Jesus sends his disciples out to preach and heal; later they return. In between, while the disciples are out on their first mission, Mark's gospel tells the story of the beheading of John the Baptist, Jesus' forerunner. John's martyrdom foreshadows the ultimate cost of Jesus' mission for him and his disciples. Like meat in a sandwich the middle story gives the surrounding story deeper meaning.

Similarly, shortly before the last supper and passion, a woman anoints Jesus on the head with costly oil the way Israel anointed its kings. Her story must be told whenever Jesus' story is told, the narrative insists. Her action is the meat of another sandwich. Immediately before the anointing is a scene in which officials decide to stop Jesus; immediately after the anointing is the scene in which Judas goes to betray Jesus. In the middle the anointing prophetically affirms Jesus' messianic identity as his passion is about to begin.

Mark's gospel not only uses literary sandwiches, its plot in chapters four to eleven includes three story cycles from oral tradition. Double stories alert us to these cycles—two sea crossings, two feeding miracles, and two healings of blind men. These twice-told stories indicate oral parentheses, one story marking the beginning of a sequence and the repetition marking its end. Oral tradition has arranged these cycles deliberately for effect just as a chef might arrange food chunks on a skewer in a pattern; for example, two pineapple chunks, then two watermelon chunks to create contrast; or, pineapple, onion, zucchini, lamb, zucchini, onion, pineapple to create symmetry.

Distinctively Mark's gospel is famous for one special motif: the messianic secret. Hearers and readers tap into this major theological motif when they wonder why Jesus cautions the leper he heals in chapter one not to tell anyone what happened. Is Jesus using reverse psychology? Does he fear sudden fame? Why keep Jesus' messianic identity secret when verse one lets the cat out of the bag right off with its proclamation, "Here begins the good news of Jesus Christ, the Son of God?" Like every narrative worth the telling, Mark's gospel pulls us to read on and find out what happens next and in the end. Many notice that Jesus gives the same warning to keep what he does secret to others he heals. A theme recurs for a reason. If we explore all the places this theme occurs, what will we find? What is the secret? Who keeps it? Who tells? How does the secret function as part of the whole? These questions stretch across the gospel narrative. In this distinguishing characteristic, scholars questing to recover the historical Jesus first recognized Mark's gospel is not a history but a literary composition deliberately and artfully constructed to engage its readers and invite us to faith in Jesus. Taking a look at the whole story will enrich and deepen readers' insights into its parts.

TOOLS FOR STUDYING THE WHOLE STORY

The way oral tradition and the gospel writer have constructed the gospel narrative expresses the theology and insights of the earliest Christians. These witnesses have sent their claims about who Jesus is to us in narrative form. To discover that the gospel is more than a story telling how things happened, readers must notice the way scenes fit together for deliberate theological effect. Here are the literary tools the approach in this book uses. Readers can use these tools or simply appreciate the approach at work in the chapters.

1 **Read the section of the gospel each chapter addresses. Divide it into scenes; even give them titles.** Record the number of verses in the scenes. A new scene begins with a change of location, topic, character, time, action. For example, in Mark 1.9-11, John the Baptist baptizes Jesus in the Jordan. In Mark 1.12-13, the Spirit drives Jesus into the wilderness—a change of character, the Holy Spirit; a change of location, the wilderness.

   Analyze what you observe. Are scenes short, long, uniform in size? What does size point to as important? For example, what is the effect of many short scenes or a long scene?

2 **What does the beginning and end of the whole gospel or the beginning and end of story strands emphasize?** These are the two best places in a narrative to make the main point.

3 **Look for how the oral storytellers and gospel writer arrange the story scenes.** Look for contrast, symmetry, parallels, juxtaposition (back to back), repetitions, steps.

4 **Notice repeated imagery** (motifs), such as the messianic secret or references to the Son of Man imagery from Daniel 7.14.

This book will aid individuals or groups who want to study Mark's gospel as a whole and explore how the narrative expresses theology. For small Christian communities and RCIA groups that use the Sunday gospels for reflection, this book will put Sunday gospel passages in their full context and take readers beyond the story into its theology.

An easy way to use the book is:

● Read and reflect on the section of the gospel cited at the beginning of each chapter.

● Read the chapter in *Mark's Gospel, the Whole Story*.

● Reflect on and discuss the questions at the end of the chapter, which aim to prompt insights and/or help you to articulate your own insights and share them.

CHAPTER 1

The Beginning and the Ending

"Here begins the good news of Jesus Christ, the Son of God" (Mark 1.1).

READ MARK 1.1 AND 16.1-20.

Verse 1 of Mark's gospel proclaims the good news its final verse leaves untold. The best ancient manuscripts end with Mary Magdalene, Mary the mother of James and Joses, and Salome standing before the empty tomb, trembling and *ecstatic*, the word literally means *beside themselves.* In the final verse the three women say nothing because they are afraid (16.8). The narrative freezes them in an awestruck tableau at the ultimate threshold of faith—the empty tomb.

So many hearers have found this suspended ending unsatisfactory that Mark's gospel has accumulated three alternative endings in its manuscript sources—a Shorter Ending, a Longer Ending, and an apocalyptic ending cited only in footnotes. In addition, both Matthew and Luke create fuller endings and include appearances of Jesus risen.

The Shorter Ending adds just two sentences. The women suspended in silent awe and ecstasy follow through on the young man's commission. **"And all that had been commanded them, they told briefly to those around Peter. And afterward Jesus himself sent out through them, from east to west, the sacred and imperishable proclamation of eternal salvation."**

The Longer Ending, Mark 16.9-20, repeats in summary form Jesus' Easter appearances from Luke's gospel. Verse 9 repeats the early morning setting and identifies Mary Magdalene as the one from whom Jesus casts out seven demons. Only Luke identifies her this way (Luke 8.2). Verses 10-11 describe the risen Jesus appearing to Mary Magdalene and her report to the other disciples, who refuse to believe her. Verses 12-13 tell a one-line version of Luke's Emmaus story, in which two disciples meet the risen Jesus on the road. Like Mary Magdalene, they tell the others, who refuse to believe them. Only in verses 14-20 does the risen Jesus appear to the eleven apostles, who then finally believe. Jesus upbraids them for their lack of faith and stubbornness and commissions them **"to preach the good news to the whole of creation"** (15). This more "satisfactory" ending gives the Eleven the authority as eyewitnesses to proclaim Jesus' resurrection from the dead and then commissions them to preach. It also includes signs of faith disturbing today—picking up deadly snakes and drinking poison without harm. The Longer Ending ends with an ascension in verses 19-20, again adding the story only Luke tells both at the end of his gospel and at the beginning of its sequel, the Acts of the Apostles.

In addition to the Shorter and Longer Endings, some manuscripts have a third ending that is apocalyptic in tone. It appears in footnotes in bibles today. In this ending Christ announces Satan's time is over.

Both Matthew and Luke use Mark's gospel narrative but both take the story farther. Matthew adds an earthquake and an angel rather than a young man in the tomb. Mary Magdalene and the other Mary hear from the angel that Jesus has been raised from the dead and is going ahead of them into Galilee. The women meet the risen Jesus on the way when they set out in joy from the tomb to tell the other disciples. Jesus himself commissions the women to tell his brothers he will see them in Galilee. Luke's gospel includes the three scenes that the Longer Ending of Mark borrows, namely, first, the women who find the tomb empty; second, the two disciples who encounter Jesus on the way to Emmaus; and third, Peter and the whole company to whom Jesus appears as they gather to report their experiences.

In earlier eras Christians have tried to harmonize Mark, Matthew, and Luke into one story. Today scholars value the distinct versions, and by valuing the differences, create a history of the early Christian communities that is more diverse. In all the best manuscripts, Mark's gospel ends at 16.8, in which the women say nothing because they are afraid.

If we readers value the original ending of Mark's gospel, we recognize the end is also a beginning: a literary threshold that invites hearers and readers to faith, the faith in Jesus that Mark's gospel proclaims in its first verse. Jesus is the *Christ* or *messiah*, the word *Christ* means the anointed one. Israel enthroned its kings by anointing them with oil on the head. Psalm 2, a prayer used as part of the king's enthronement, hails a new king in verse 10, "You are my son; today I have begotten you." Calling Jesus both the Christ and the Son of God in verse one affirms doubly he is Israel's messiah. The good news begins with Jesus and continues in the faith of his disciples in every generation. The first verse announces the beginning of a new day in creation: life in the light of Jesus' resurrection from the dead.

1   What is the good news Mark 1.1 announces?

2   What questions does the original ending of Mark's gospel at 16.8 raise for you?

3   How is the beginning of Mark's gospel really the ending?

4   What effects do each of the three alternative endings create as you read them? What do you find at stake— gained and lost—in each ending?

5   More than once Mark's gospel suspends the action as it does at the end or leaves rhetorical questions hanging in the air. Notice the dramatic and theological impact these silences have on you as a gospel reader, as one for whom this gospel was written.

CHAPTER 2

John the Baptist and Jesus, Prophets

Mark 1.2-13

READ MARK 1.2-13.

In all four gospels John the Baptist has an unassailable place as Jesus' precursor. His preaching and baptizing attract crowds and ready people to open their ears and hearts to God. Christian tradition compares his voice to that of the prophet Second Isaiah, who around 540 B.C. called the exiled Israelites to see in the victories of the Persian King Cyrus over the Babylonians the hand of their God preparing to lead them home. Just as this prophetic voice in Isaiah 40-55 called Israel to prepare the way of the Holy One, so the Baptist prepares Jesus' way.

The Baptist wears a camel hair garment and leather belt; he eats locusts and honey. His clothing and diet identify him as a person able to survive in the wilderness. We infer desert solitude has scoured his spirit and necessitated simplicity.

The garment likens the Baptist to Elijah, the troubler of Israel, who stood alone against the faithless king Ahab and his Canaanite wife Jezebel, dueled with the prophets of Baal about who could make it rain, and then, fed by ravens, escaped to Mt. Sinai. Elijah found no divine presence in lightning and storm at the holy mountain but instead heard God speaking within—in the silence of his interior consciousness. So holy is Elijah that he doesn't die. God carries him off to heaven in a fiery chariot.

By identifying John the Baptist with the voice of Second Isaiah and a fiery prophetic figure like Elijah, the gospel places Jesus in the long line of Israel's prophets who put their lives on the line to speak for God to the kings. Mark's gospel provides no formal genealogy for Jesus but evokes this prophetic lineage.

Christian tradition remembers John for preaching conversion and baptizing those who want to change their lives. The gospels place Jesus among the crowds of spiritual seekers who receive John's baptism. All four gospels repeat the same formula to describe the relationship between Jesus and the Baptist, who insists, **"One more powerful than I is coming after me. I am not worthy to stoop and untie his sandals. I have baptized you with water but he will baptize you with the Holy Spirit"** (1.7-8).

THE BAPTISM OF JESUS AND TESTING TIME

His baptism identifies Jesus as God's Son and servant and initiates his public ministry. The baptism scene works like an icon with key symbols to draw us into its portrait of who Jesus is. He is not alone in his mission but lives in the embrace of Father and Spirit.

Jesus sees the heavens split open as he comes out of the water after John baptizes him. *Schizo* is the word in the original Greek, which translates in English *split* or *torn apart* as in the English word *schism*. A new relationship between heaven and earth begins in Jesus.

From the heavens the Spirit descends upon Jesus like a dove. In Genesis 1.2 the Spirit hovers like a bird over the waters of the deep, stirring them into new form. In coming upon Jesus, the Spirit begins a new creation. The descent of the Spirit upon Jesus is also an anointing. Isaiah promises Israel's faithful God will one day anoint a great leader with God's own Spirit rather than oil (Isaiah 11.1-2). This Spirit-filled leader is the messiah whose reign will bring justice and peace. The coming of the Spirit upon Jesus anoints him for the ministry of revealing God's love in healing and freeing humankind.

The voice that speaks from heaven proclaims Jesus is **"my beloved Son."** The tender words **"beloved"** and **"in you I am well pleased"** echo Isaiah 42.1-4, 6-7, a passage that describes the people of Israel in exile as God's beloved servant. The people in exile make their God known among the nations. Their return from exile teaches them the transcendent Creator God who made a path to freedom through the sea can make a smooth road to lead them home through the wilderness. In Jesus, God's servant and Son, God is at work in the world anew.

After the baptism the Spirit next drives Jesus into the desert, and Satan tests him for 40 days. The 40 days suggest Israel's 40 years in the desert, a time of closeness and dependence on God. The gospel tells us this solitude leads

Jesus to preach God's nearness, gather disciples, free people from demons, and heal the sick. But Mark's gospel leaves largely to our imaginations all that these two dynamic verbs, *drives* and *tests*, imply. Mark's gospel has no extended conversation between Jesus and Satan as Matthew and Luke do. However, in Mark 3.20-30 scribes accuse Jesus of acting in the power of Satan rather than the power of the Holy Spirit. Jesus asks, **"How can Satan cast out Satan?"** He insists every sin is forgivable except blasphemy against the Holy Spirit. In relation to a human being, to blaspheme is to defame, slander, and revile a person, to smear and abuse them with words. In relation to God, to blaspheme is to speak irreverently, sacrilegiously. Blasphemous words, even against God, are forgivable. To blaspheme against the Holy Spirit is to deny one's own interior, animating spirit, one's own experience of the Holy Spirit within. Today we might call this going against one's conscience, the place where we make our most defining choice for good or evil. Clearly during the first days of his ministry Jesus demonstrates in his healing, forgiving actions the good news the Spirit drives him to bring among the people of Galilee.

1 What do you appreciate about seeing Jesus in the line of Israel's prophets?

2 What does the scene of Jesus' baptism tell you about who he is?

3 How does solitude test you? What is its value for you?

4 How does the early Christians' use of the Hebrew scriptures help and hinder you in reading Mark's gospel?

CHAPTER 3

Jesus' First Days of Ministry Stir Controversy
Mark 1.14-3.35

READ MARK 1.14-3.35.

In Mark's gospel Jesus begins his ministry when he hears the Baptist has been arrested. His first words announce the profound significance of his ministry and person. **"God's reign is near."** In Jesus' coming among the people of Galilee, God's promises have ripened into fulfillment. Jesus' message is a call: **"Repent and believe the good news"** (1.15).

The word *repent* in Greek is *metanoia,* which means *conversion—turning around* or *toward* or *back.* Jesus' call goes beyond John the Baptist's call to a baptism of repentance and forgiveness of sin. Jesus invites faith in him and his good news. He is the one to follow.

After establishing the theme of Jesus' preaching, the gospel narrative sets Jesus in furious motion. Mark's stories are short; the gospel writer uses the word *immediately* to shift quickly to new scenes. With Jesus' every step, God's dynamic, healing, liberating power breaks into the human community.

In these opening three chapters Jesus preaches, calls disciples, heals people, casts out demons, forgives sins, appoints the Twelve, and claims those who do the will of God as his real family. Frequently the gospel writer follows a scene in which Jesus heals one person with a scene in which he heals many. He calls one tax collector; many come to dinner. Jesus' fame spreads; crowds swell with travelers from increasing distances; scribes and Pharisees accuse him of breaking the law and blaspheming.

DAY ONE: FRIDAY ALONG THE SHORE

Immediately after his baptism and Spirit time in the desert, Jesus appears in Galilee. It's a Friday as Jesus strides along the lakeshore, sees Peter and Andrew fishing, and calls them to follow him. **"Come after me. I will make you fishers of people"** (1.17). Immediately the two follow. Jesus walks on and sees James and John readying their nets and calls out to them. Immediately and without good reason James and John leave their father and go off with Jesus. The four unhesitatingly take first steps into new lives. Jesus' call is direct; their responses quick and decisive. However, their maturing as committed disciples happens more slowly. Only gradually as they accompany Jesus do they appreciate who he is. Their fear, incomprehension, and flight make them ideal role models for us readers who like them fail and flee Jesus' call. Their story is part of Jesus' story from the beginning.

DAY TWO: SABBATH IN CAPERNAUM

Jesus headquarters his ministry in Capernaum on the north shore of the Sea of Galilee. On Sabbath Jesus preaches at the local synagogue; his new disciples go with him. The dark basalt foundation of this synagogue still rests beneath the ruins of a second-century synagogue that stands at the highest point in the village. What amazes those who hear Jesus preach is the authority he claims. He does not cite the legal precedents of the oral and written law as was apparently the practice of the scribes and Pharisees. He challenges the law in a sense that amazes and attracts his hearers.

A man shouts out to Jesus in the synagogue; an ungodly spirit possesses the man the way success, security, drugs, alcohol can drive any of us. Ironically this unclean spirit, recognizing a threat in Jesus, is the first to proclaim, **"I know who you are—the Holy One of God"** (1.24). Jesus will not allow this voice to herald who he is. Jesus silences the spirit and frees the man from its influence. Jesus' action elevates his hearers' response from interest to amazement and creates the first of many thresholds in the gospel where faith can begin. **"What is this?"** the people ask and answer, **"A new teaching—with authority!"** People talk; Jesus becomes famous.

From the synagogue, Jesus and his four disciples go to Peter's house, where his mother-in-law lies sick with a fever. **"Jesus took her by the hand and lifted her up. The fever left her and she began to serve them"** (1.31). The word *lift* in English, *egeiro* in

Greek, means *to raise up*. This is the same verb Jesus uses when he predicts his passion, **"After I am raised up, I will go before you into Galilee"** (14.28). The young man uses the same verb when he tells the three woman who find the tomb empty, **"He has been raised; he is not here"** (16.6). Mark's gospel uses the same word to describe Jesus' healing actions and God's action in Jesus' resurrection.

Peter's mother-in-law becomes Jesus' first woman disciple. Her story takes just one verse among the 660 verses in Mark's gospel. She responds to Jesus lifting her up by serving him. The Greek word *diakonie* means *serve*. It can mean providing for physical needs and serving the table. In fact, the New American Bible translates her response, "she began to wait on them." The English word *deacon* comes from this same Greek word. The work of serving the tables later becomes an office in the Christian community (Acts 6.1-6).

In Mark's gospel Jesus says of himself, **"the Son of Man came not to be served but to serve and to give his life as a ransom for many"** (10.45). If we apply this definition to Peter's mother-in-law, she responds to her healing by giving her life to the new community. In fact in the story the male disciples and Jesus come to be served; she is the model disciple who serves.

DAY THREE: THE MISSION WIDENS

After sunset, a new day begins. Sick and possessed people crowd Jesus door. He heals and frees them, repeating for many what he has done for two individuals, the man in the synagogue and Peter's mother-in-law. This is Mark's storytelling technique. The first evangelist dramatizes the dynamic inbreaking of God's healing, liberating power in Jesus' ministry by following two stories in which Jesus helps individuals with a summary scene in which he helps many.

After a little time in the evening to sit apart from the crowds and pray, his disciples find Jesus and they set off to bring the good news to surrounding villages.

With Jesus' widening mission, the narrative stops marking days. Interestingly Mark's gospel begins and ends with the same three days—Friday, Sabbath, Sunday. In the first three Jesus gathers disciples, heals the sick, frees the possessed, bringing God's kin*dom near.

Chapter one ends with the story of a leper who can't keep secret who Jesus is and spreads his fame. The leper so moves Jesus to pity that he stretches out his hand, touches, and heals the man but tells him **"to say nothing to anyone"** (1.44). Jesus demonstrates the wholeness God intends for human beings and returns the man to the life of the human community. This person isolated by his disease from family and neighbors cannot contain his good news. He **"went out and proclaimed the matter freely."** He becomes the first of four suppliants who won't keep the secret of who Jesus is. The leper testifies to all Jesus has done for him.

CONTROVERSIES BEGIN

After reading the first chapter of Mark, we expect Jesus to preach the good news, heal the sick, and free the possessed. He travels to other villages to do what he does in Capernaum. When he returns, increasing numbers crowd his house and door (2.1). In fact, four men have to dig through the roof to lower a paralyzed friend into Jesus' presence.

To readers' surprise, Jesus forgives the paralyzed man's sins rather than healing his body. Jesus does what only God can do. Scribes take notice. Jesus takes them on, **"Which is easier, to say to this paralyzed man, 'Your sins are forgiven,' or to say, 'Stand up, take your mat, and walk?'"** Then Jesus demonstrates his authority to forgive sins by saying to the man, **"Arise, take up your mat, and go home"** (2.11). Immediately he does.

This story is longer than any other in the first three chapters. It is a literary and theological sandwich that introduces controversy into the narrative. Jesus' forgiving action forms the top and his healing action the bottom of the sandwich; the theological controversy about which is easier, forgiving or healing, is the meat in the middle.

Mark's gospel narrates three more controversies between Jesus and the religious authorities in chapter two. In each tension heightens. In Mark 2.16 the scribes question Jesus' disciples about why he eats with sinners. In Mark 2.24 they question Jesus directly about why he and his disciples pick grain on Sabbath. These controversies about the law culminate in a plot to accuse and destroy Jesus in Mark 3.2, 6.

Jesus does not duck controversy and extends his ministry to people outside the law. Levi is sitting in his tax collection booth when Jesus calls him to become a disciple. By calling Levi, Jesus includes in his inner circle a person the Pharisees regard as a threat to Jewish identity, a person outside the law because he collaborates with the Romans and collects their taxes. Levi is not the only tax collector who follows Jesus. When Jesus and his disciples eat at Levi's house, many tax collectors and sinners join them, **"for there were many who followed him"** (2.15).

Jesus continues gathering disciples and appoints twelve to become apostles, whom he sends out with authority to proclaim the message and cast out demons. As chapter three ends, his family and mother go to see Jesus in Capernaum (3.31). People are telling them he is out of his mind. When his family asks to see him, Jesus does not go out to them but says, **"Whoever does the will of God is my brother and sister and mother"**(3.35). Jesus claims his followers rather than his relatives as his family. Jesus does in these first days what he does in all his days—preach, heal, cast out demons, gather followers, forgive sins, and generate controversy.

1 What sense of who Jesus is do you get from the fast and furious pace in his first days of ministry? What sense of Jesus' identity emerges? Who do you imagine Jesus thinks he is?

2 How do you interpret the gospel's use of *egeiro* for Jesus' actions in his miracles and in God's raising him to new life?

3 In what sense do Jesus' first days tell the whole story of his ministry?

4 Imagine what Peter's mother-in-law's life is like after Jesus raises her up, and she becomes his disciple, serving him and the community he is gathering.

5 What is the kin*dom Jesus brings near? How do you experience it today?

6 Who belongs to the family Jesus claims as his own (Mark 3.31-35)? Who are those that do the will of God and are brothers, sisters, and mother to Jesus? Who belongs in an illustration of this scene?

CHAPTER 4

Sowing the Word: A Hundredfold Promise

Mark 4.1-34

READ MARK 4.1-34.

By chapter four of Mark's gospel Jesus' fame has so spread that he resorts to preaching from a boat for crowd control. His disciples have the boat ready (3.9). He sits in the boat; the crowd listens on shore.

Jesus teaches in open-ended parables rather than imperatives or stories with familiar morals. Jesus' parables invite hearers to make their own judgments. Parables work like mirrors in which hearers can see themselves and reflect on the consequences of their judgments. In this teaching style people participate in their own learning. People remember and apply parables to new situations or gain new insights from the judgments they make. Parables respect our human capacity to think and choose.

Large crowds see and hear Jesus teach in parables but without understanding. The gospel writer creates a narrative sandwich that invites us readers to become insiders with Jesus' disciples and learn the secret meaning of the parable. Between teaching the parable of the sower to the crowd (4.1-9) and interpreting the parable for his disciples (4.13-20), Jesus gathers his inner circle, the twelve, to reflect on the mystery of the kin*dom of God. In this meaty middle Jesus quotes God's ironic words to the prophet Isaiah, warning him that his preaching will fail, "Go, say to the people, 'Keep listening but do not comprehend; keep looking but do not understand.'" God makes Isaiah's charge the opposite of its real prophetic purpose:

> *"Make the mind of this people dull,*
> *and stop their ears,*
> *and shut their eyes,*
> *so that they may not look with their eyes*
> *and listen with their ears*
> *and comprehend with their minds, and turn,*
> *and be healed" (Isaiah 6.9-10).*

The messianic secret is about more than keeping Jesus' healing, freeing actions from spreading his fame. It is about more than reverse psychology. It is about the mystery of the human encounter with the divine, the human heart and free will. A prophet's words do not always take root and yield fruit as the parable of the sower promises. The disciples who follow Jesus are living into the mystery of God's kin*dom. For others, the parables remain stories but not mirrors that lead to insight into the holy or the self. The gospel privileges us readers as insiders who comprehend the whole post-Easter story, in fact the whole 2,000-year story of abundant yield.

The interpretation of the sower parable describes the seed falling onto four kinds of ground—a path where the birds eat it, rocky ground where the seeds spring up quickly but the sun shrivels the plants; a thorny patch where weeds choke out the grain; and good ground where the seed yields abundantly. This interpretation becomes a parable in itself that invites further interpretation. Are most people typically one kind of ground or are we these various kinds of ground at different times in our lives; for example, sometimes pulled by work and worry away from God's presence?

Some connect Peter with the rocky ground; he is the first to profess Jesus is the messiah but then denies him. Ultimately Peter becomes good ground. His post-Easter faith roots deep, multiples a hundredfold in his preaching, and endures in the face of martyrdom.

Despite the possibility that few will understand and turn toward God, Mark's gospel makes the sower a parable of promise. On good ground the word of God yields thirty, sixty, and a hundredfold, a promise that extends beyond Jesus' death and resurrection and across the centuries (4.20).

After the four kinds of ground, the narrative attaches sayings loosely connected to the parable of the sower and its interpretation. The first saying anticipates a post-Easter perspective. **"There is nothing hidden, except to be disclosed; nor is anything secret, except to come to light"** (4.22). The second saying addresses the mystery of our openness to the word. **"Pay attention to what you hear; the measure you give will be the measure you get, and still more will be given you"** (4.24).

Two additional short parables conclude this parable section of Mark's gospel. Like seeds scattered in the ground that grow in the night while the farmer sleeps, the kin*dom of God has a dynamic of its own (4.26-29). The smallest of seeds can grow into the largest of shrubs and provide nests for birds in its shade (4.30-32). These are parables of promise. We live our lives in the midst of the wonder of growth and the promise of Jesus' self-giving death and life-giving resurrection.

1 What ruts, rocks, and thorns keep the word of God from bearing fruit in your life?

2 Why do you think Mark places the parable of the sower early in the gospel narrative?

3 What do you think the first audiences of Mark's gospel in A.D. 70 would hear in the parable of the sower? What do you hear in the parable today?

4 Where do you see the abundant yield the sower parable promises?

5 What experience do you have, if any, of seeing but not perceiving, listening but not understanding?

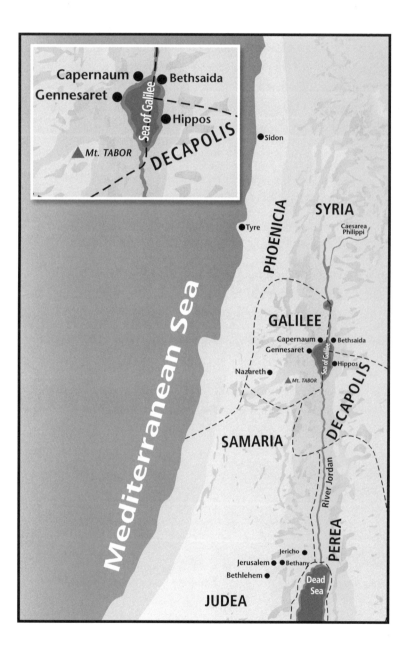

CHAPTER 5

A Community at Sea:
Called From Fear to Faith
Mark 4.35-6.33; 6.45-51

READ MARK 4.35-6.33; 6.45-6.51.

The audience for whom Mark writes the first gospel fears the future and faces a crisis—how will Jesus' message and mission continue as the eyewitness generation passes from history? The Romans lay siege to Jerusalem to put down the Jewish rebellion that began in A.D. 66. The Christian community in the city flees to Galilee. The siege leaves not one stone of the temple upon another but also destroys religious practice as Jews knew it in Jesus' time. Synagogues replace temple worship and sacrifices. No more will Jews stream up the roads to celebrate Passover or Pentecost in Jerusalem. Christian Jews now have no place of worship in common with other Jews. The ancient religion ends; both modern Judaism and Christianity develop out of this tradition.

FIRST SEA CROSSING
MARK 4.35-41

Sea crossings begin and end the story strand in chapters 4.35-6.51. At Jesus' suggestion in the first sea crossing, the disciples are going from Galilee to the other side, the name for the eastern, Gentile side of the Sea of Galilee, the Decapolis area. A boat full of disciples gives us an image of Church, of communities of faith. The disciples are at sea, in a transition, between one shore and another, one era and another. Jesus is asleep in the boat. A terrible squall arises, threatening to capsize the boat. The disciples fear for their lives and awaken Jesus, who calms the waves and asks, **"Why are you afraid? Have you still no faith?"** (4.40).

This story raises a key question for every generation. How do we move from fear to faith or from doubt to faith? How do we navigate the stormy seas of our times and travel from a certain past to a future we participate in making but cannot see? The hearers for whom Mark writes in A.D. 70 know Jesus' eyewitness disciples, such as Peter, James, and John, as mature and committed Christians, not as the fearful, bewildered, awed, confused disciples who lived through Jesus' hope-dashing death and mind-boggling resurrection. Mark wants his hearers to recognize that they are where Jesus' disciples were at the beginning of their ministry—afraid, amazed, often confused.

When Jesus calms the sea, his disciples move from fear for their lives to awe. Mark suspends the story with the disciples expressing their awe in a rhetorical question, **"Who is this that even the wind and sea obey him?"** (4.41).

A rhetorical question implies an answer so obvious that it doesn't need to be said. The rhetorical question creates a threshold for the hearer of the gospel who can answer the question the narrative suspends in silence. Awe is the beginning of wisdom, the Old Testament Wisdom books say repeatedly. For Mark awe is a liminal experience, a threshold or open doorway to faith and commitment.

A GERASENE PREACHER
MARK 5.1-20

The second story in the narrative strand takes place on the other side of the sea in the country of the Gerasenes. Immediately a man with an unclean spirit approaches Jesus. The man lives shackled among the tombs until he breaks loose; no one can subdue him. He howls and bruises himself. As he bows before Jesus, his legion of demons speaks and acknowledges Jesus as Son of the Most High God. The man assumes Jesus can help him but pleads with Jesus not to send these ungodly spirits out into the countryside. Jesus sends them into a herd of swine instead. The swineherds report what has happened. Gerasenes quickly arrive to see and grow afraid. They beg Jesus to leave their neighborhood.

The man Jesus frees of unclean spirits and restores to his right mind wants to become a disciple and travel with Jesus. Instead Jesus commissions him, **"Go home to your friends, and tell them how much the Lord has done for you."** The man **"began to preach in the Decapolis how much Jesus has done for him; and everyone was amazed"** (5.20). This nameless suppliant is the second person in the gospel to tell people who Jesus is, to proclaim the secret. His hearers respond with amazement; his preaching creates for them a threshold of faith. Jesus and his disciples return to Galilee.

TWO DAUGHTERS
MARK 5.21-43

A story within a story forms the heart of this long narrative strand. In this literary sandwich a man named Jairus approaches Jesus to heal his daughter who is gravely ill. On the way to help the girl, a woman with a hemorrhage touches Jesus; her story interrupts the story of Jairus' daughter, which continues after the woman's healing.

Both stories are about daughters. The girl is 12, a daughter of Jairus and of the synagogue he leads. Jesus addresses the woman who has hemorrhaged for 12 years as his daughter after she tells the whole truth of her healing. **"But the woman, knowing what had happened to her, came in fear and trembling, fell down before him, and told him the whole truth"** (5.33). She becomes a daughter of his new community—a believer.

Twelve is an important number in both stories. The girl is the approximate age for the onset of menstruation. The woman has suffered a flow of her lifeblood for 12 years and for all these years has been unable to worship in the temple. Leviticus 15.19-31 says that a flow of blood makes a woman unclean, contaminates anyone she touches, and prevents her from entering and defiling the temple. In the case of the hemorrhaging woman, the opposite occurs. Her touch doesn't make Jesus unclean; instead it heals her and makes her whole.

Mark and the oral tradition he writes down connects these two stories with Jesus' own story. The Greek word *mastigos*, which names the flow of blood, labels it a *scourge*. In Acts 22.24 and Hebrews 11.36 this word refers to floggings and scourgings. The word connotes suffering like Jesus' own in his passion and death. Seeking out Jesus is the last desperate act of the woman with the hemorrhage. Doctors have failed her. She has spent her resources. Her condition has worsened. The woman's lifeblood keeps hemorrhaging from her body just as Jesus' lifeblood pours out in his suffering and death.

The woman takes matters into her own hands and touches Jesus' garment, not him directly. Her gesture is significant and symbolic. The people for whom Mark writes in A.D. 70 will meet Jesus in story and sacrament, at a distance rather than face to face like the eyewitnesses. In her story the woman healed of hemorrhage moves from desperation, to fear and trembling, and then to testifying to the whole truth of what has happened to her. She proclaims the good news of her healing publicly in the midst of the crowd. Jesus affirms, **"Daughter, your faith has healed you"** (5.34). She becomes the third of only four people in Mark's gospel who proclaim who Jesus is, who tell the secret.

Jairus and his wife experience parents' worst fear—that their daughter will die. Like the terrified disciples in the boat Jairus begs Jesus for help. The story of the hemorrhaging woman interrupts and delays Jesus' response to Jairus, so the girl worsens and dies. The literary sandwich continues as Jesus invites Jairus to move from fear to faith. **"Do not fear, only believe"** (5.36). Jesus heals the girl in private with her parents and three disciples—Peter, James, and John. Jesus takes the girl by the hand and says, **"Talitha cum. Little girl, arise"** (5.41). The gospel again uses word *egeiro*, (*arise*) just as it does in describing Jesus raising up Peter's mother-in-law and his own resurrection. Peter, James, and John witness this miracle but keep it secret as Jesus commands.

The woman's story emphasizes a long-time bloody suffering; the girl's story is a resurrection story. Together the stories identify with Jesus' suffering and resurrection.

The woman's witness is at the heart of this story strand (Mark 4.35-6.51), which follows the pattern A, B, C, D, C1, B1, A1. The sea crossing is the first story; it leaves Jesus' disciples in awe (A). Freeing the man of a legion of unclean spirits and commissioning him to preach to his own people is the second story. His people, the Gentile Gerasenes, fear Jesus and beg him to leave their area (B). Jairus seeks Jesus' help in the third story (C) before the woman with the hemorrhage interrupts, the fourth story (D). She is a Jewish woman who like the man freed of unclean spirits becomes a preacher among her own people. Both tell who Jesus is. Both model faith that gives witness and builds up the community in A.D. 70. The raising of Jairus's daughter continues the third story and begins reversing the plot (C1).

NAZARENES REJECT JESUS
MARK 6.1-6.

Next Jesus preaches in his hometown; the people of Nazareth reject him. **"Many who hear Jesus preach are astounded and ask, 'Where did this man get all this? What is this wisdom**

that has been given to him'" (6.2)? The Nazarenes are certain they know who Jesus is. **"Isn't this the carpenter, the son of Mary and the brother of James, Joses, Judas, and Simon— and aren't his sisters here with us as well"** (6.3)? Like the Garazenes who beg Jesus to leave their area (B), the Nazarenes reject Jesus (B1). They take offense. Jesus can do no deeds of power except heal a few people. His teaching in Nazareth leaves Jesus **"amazed at their unbelief"** rather than anyone amazed at him (6.6). The Nazarenes reject Jesus, his wisdom, and his mighty deeds. What blocks the people's hearing in Nazareth is certainty and cynicism. They are too certain who Jesus is to listen one another into new perceptions.

THE COST OF DISCIPLESHIP
MARK 6.7-33

At this point in the story strand the narrative introduces another literary sandwich, another story within a story. The narrative delays the second sea crossing story and adds a literary sandwich focused on mission. In the first slice of story Jesus sends his disciples out to do what he has been doing—preach, heal, cast out ungodly spirits (E). While the new missionaries are out, the narrative ominously tells the story of the beheading of John the Baptist (F). The Baptist's beheading supplies time for the twelve to be out on mission. More importantly, John's senseless death at the whimsy of a drunken king foreshadows the cost of prophetic ministry. What happens to John may happen to Jesus and those who follow him. Jesus' disciples and those Mark's gospel calls to faith have reason to fear for their lives. The disciples return and report to Jesus all they have done but cannot find rest even when they go away with Jesus in a boat to a deserted place (E1). The Jesus movement keeps growing.

SECOND SEA CROSSING
MARK 6.45-51

Finally then Mark's gospel arrives at the second sea crossing story (A1). However, before the cycle wraps up, the narrative begins the next cycle of stories, interlocking the feeding miracle strand with the sea-crossing strand to create a continuous narrative. After their mission Jesus takes his disciples away to the deserted place along the north shore where they seek rest from the crowds of people who need healing and where Jesus feeds 5,000. After the feeding the disciples take the boat and row east toward Bethsaida. Jesus stays behind to pray.

The disciples row all night against a strong wind. Jesus sees this and comes toward them walking on the sea. He intends to pass them by. The disciples think they are seeing a ghost, which terrifies them. They don't recognize Jesus. Jesus relieves their fears, **"Take heart; it is I. Do not be afraid."** The disciples move from terror to amazement but not to faith. The multiplication of the loaves has bewildered them. In fact, the gospel uses the terminology from Isaiah and explains, **"Their hearts were hardened"** (6.52). Their feelings lead into the next story cycle.

With the sending out of Jesus' disciples, the narrative anticipates their post-resurrection mission to the world. With the beheading of the Baptist, the narrative reaches back into the past and connects Jesus' mission with the line of Israel's prophets. A Gentile man and a Jewish woman, both nameless suppliants, testify to all Jesus has done for them, modeling new sources of leadership for Mark's audience in A.D. 70

1 What lies on either shore for the Christians for whom Mark writes in A.D. 70? What lies on either shore for Christians today?

2 The Gerasene leaders react to Jesus with fear. The people of Nazareth reject him. What makes believing easier for some and riskier for others? What is riskier—certainty or newness?

3 What is awe? When have you experienced feelings of awe and amazement? What is the wisdom that begins in awe?

4 With whom in this section of the gospel do you identify?

5 What significance for interpreting the whole cycle do you find in the two pivotal stories—the woman with the hemorrhage and the beheading of John the Baptist? What insights does this whole section bring to you today?

Artist/Sadao Watanabe

CHAPTER 6

Bread For All:
"Do you understand?"

Mark 6.34-44; 6.52-8.21

READ MARK 6.34-44; 6.52-8.21.

Most Christian bible readers credit Paul of Tarsus with initiating a full scale mission to Gentiles. Paul makes three journeys through Asia Minor, on to Greek cities, and the seat of Roman Empire, Rome. Amazingly in Mark's gospel, Jesus undertakes his own mission to the Gentiles in the strand of stories between the two feeding miracles. Geography is crucial and confusing in this segment of oral tradition. The first feeding takes place in Jewish territory. The second sea crossing interrupts, but the disciples stay along the north shore of the Sea of Galilee. After the crossing, the feeding story strand resumes and with Jesus aboard, the disciples land in Gennesaret, a Jewish village on the northwest side of the lake (6.43). From there Jesus leaves Galilee to go to Tyre, a Gentile city on the Mediterranean coast, Lebanon today (7.24). Jesus stays in Gentile territory and takes a circuitous route first north from Tyre to Sidon and then south toward the Sea of Galilee and the region of the Decapolis.

FIRST FEEDING MIRACLE
MARK 6.34-44

The needs of the people animate Jesus' first feeding miracle. He feels compassion for the crowds, whom he sees as sheep without a shepherd. Jesus feeds them his teachings before he feeds them bread and fish. As the hour grows late, his disciples worry about feeding the crowds and urge Jesus to send them away so they can find food to eat. Jesus challenges his disciples, **"You give them something to eat"** (6.37). Jesus calls them to mission, but the disciples perceive the situation in dollars and cents, estimating the crowd will require 200 denarii to buy enough food. A denarius is a day's wage. Some interpreters today explain Jesus' multiplication of the loaves and fish as a miracle of generosity. They imagine people in the crowd have food. Jesus' teaching inspires them to share it. That may be but even more is happening in this account.

The disciples find five loaves and two fish among the people in the crowd. Jesus looks to heaven and does what his disciples see and hear at the last supper and what Christians to this day reenact when they gather for Eucharist: **"He looked up to heaven, and blessed and broke the loaves and gave them to his disciples to set before the crowd"** (6.41). He divides the fish among them all. Five thousand men eat and the disciples gather up twelve baskets of leftovers. The miracle ends abruptly with this count of eaters and leftovers without response from the disciples or crowd. The gospel interprets the event only after the second feeding miracle.

CROWDS SEEK HEALING
MARK 6.53-56

Crowds follow Jesus incessantly. As he and his disciples land in Gennesaret, people immediately recognize him and bring him their sick. The gospel writer provides a summary scene that vividly describes people bringing their sick to marketplaces in cities and villages, to farms. In fact, even those who touch Jesus' cloak are healed just as the woman with the hemorrhage was. This detail suggest the position of people in A.D. 70 who can no longer encounter Jesus face to face but discover the power of faith in Jesus to heal them.

CLEAN AND UNCLEAN FOOD
MARK 7.1-23

The gospel writer juxtaposes a Jewish story and a Gentile story at the center of the story strand the feeding miracles begin and end. In the Jewish story Jesus has a long discussion with Pharisees and scribes from Jerusalem about religious observance. Jesus' disciples are eating without washing their hands, a seemingly small matter but the Pharisees teach people to keep the law strictly as a source of religious identity in their Roman-occupied country. Jesus insists, **"There is nothing outside a person that by going in can defile, but the things that come out are what defile"** (7.15). Later he explains further to his disciples, **"It is what comes out of a human person that defiles. For it is from within, from the human heart, that evil intentions come: fornication, theft, murder, adultery, avarice, wickedness, deceit, licentiousness, envy, slander, pride, folly"** (7.20-22).

CRUMBS FOR GENTILES
MARK 7.24-30

Back to back with this long conversation about Jewish law, Mark's gospel tells the story of a Syrophoenician woman who will not be refused healing for her daughter. Now in Gentile territory in Tyre, Jesus enters a house and wants no one to know he is there, another instance of keeping his messianic identity secret. But Jesus doesn't escape notice. Once again a suppliant finds him. In this case, a nameless mother with Syrian and Phoenician ethnic roots comes to him, bows down, and begs him to cast the demon out of her daughter.

Jesus refuses, the only time he refuses a suppliant. In saying no, he makes a very prejudiced statement, "**Let the children be fed first, for it is not fair to take the children's food and throw it to the dogs**" (7.27). In other words his healing and freeing powers are for Jews, not Gentile dogs. Jesus' refusal expresses prejudice, not a test of faith. The gospel identifies the woman by her Syrophoenician ethnic roots. She is a representative Gentile as well as an individual suppliant in need. This story puts prejudice against Gentiles in Jesus' mouth. Both Mark's gospel and Matthew's gospel put the same, exact words in Jesus' mouth, expressing a deep cultural bias against Gentiles that the first Christians found among them. Jews regarded dogs as unclean for their propensity to dig up dead things.

The woman sasses Jesus in response. **"But she answered him, "Sir, even the dogs under the table eat the children's crumbs"** (7.28). She speaks the truth of her experience to Jesus and to all those in the early communities who used this saying to label Gentiles as dogs and keep them out of their communities. The woman gives us a glimpse into her Gentile household. Indeed she has a dog that eats the crumbs under her table. The word for dog in this story implies a small lap dog. Children and dogs have a place in this Gentile woman's kitchen and she claims a crumb of healing for her daughter from Jesus. For her saying, Jesus heals her daughter. Her words have taught the teacher. The teacher accepts a Gentile; Jesus is the voice of authority. Anyone who uses this saying to exclude Gentiles from breaking bread with them has no basis in Jesus' teachings. The Syrophoenician woman contends with a tradition that excludes her by speaking the truth of her life experience. In her retort this story strand pivots toward Jesus' Gentile mission and the second feeding miracle.

NEW GENTILE PREACHERS
MARK 7.31-37

On his circuitous tour through Gentile territory, Jesus opens the ears and frees the tongue of man who is deaf and has a speech impediment. Again, Jesus invokes the messianic secret. **"Tell no one."** However, Jesus' request can't stop this man's friends. **"The more he ordered them, the more zealously they proclaimed it"**(7.36). They become catalysts for spreading Jesus' reputation among Gentiles. **"He has done everything well; he even makes the deaf to hear and the mute to speak"** (7.37).

Freeing the Syrophoenician woman's daughter of a demon takes place in a house. Opening of the deaf man's ears happens in public with friends as witnesses. Like the leper healed (1.40-45), the Gerazene freed of demons (5.1-20), the woman cured of hemorrhage (5.25-34), this man's friends find voice as preachers of the good news.

These four preachers are the only ones in Mark's gospel who tell the secret of their healing. Each is a nameless suppliant with an affliction. Two are Jews—the leper and woman healed of hemorrhage; the Gerasene and the deaf man's friends are Gentiles. The men and women in Jesus' inner circle, such as Peter, James, John, Mary Magdalene, Mary the Mother of James and Joses, and Salome, never tell the secret in Mark's gospel even though in history the apostles preached and spread the good news of Jesus' resurrection throughout the Mediterranean area. Instead the gospel writer characterizes Peter, James, John and the other disciples in their pre-Easter mode, often confused, often in awe, but unable to perceive fully who Jesus is. At the same time the gospel writer gives these four suppliants double roles. As part of Jesus' ministry in A.D. 30, they are suppliants. For the writer's audience in A.D. 70, they are role models. Their testimony to all their faith in Jesus has done for them fuels the continuing spread of the good news.

SECOND FEEDING MIRACLE
MARK 8.1-21

In Mark's gospel Jesus himself takes his ministry to the Gentiles. In his second feeding miracle he multiples loaves and fishes among Gentiles. The two feeding miracles closely parallel one another. In both Jesus has compassion for a crowd that has come a great distance, and his disciples worry how to feed so many. In Gentile territory they find seven loaves and a few fish among the vast crowd. Jesus multiplies the seven loaves. **"He took the seven loaves and after giving thanks broke them and gave them to his disciples to distribute"** (8.6). He also blesses and distributes the fish. This time Jesus feeds 4,000 Gentiles and his disciples find seven baskets of leftovers. Like the first feeding miracle, this story ends abruptly with its count of eaters and leftovers.

The exact numbers in each case and the exact parallel of the two stories cry out for interpretation but the narrative remains silent about the meaning. It gives readers time to ponder the parallels and contrast as Jesus and the disciples set off again in the boat. The narrative does not allow them to sail away from the meaning of the miracles. On their boat trip they meet Pharisees who test Jesus by asking for a sign from heaven. Jesus sighs and says, **"No sign will be given to this generation"** (8.12). We readers recognize that in healing the sick and feeding the hungry Jesus has already revealed signs of who he is, signs the Pharisees don't perceive.

Jesus and his disciples set off again by boat, debriefing their experience of the feeding miracles. The disciples have only one loaf of bread with them. This is where the first feeding miracle started—them without bread. Jesus cautions, **"Beware the yeast of the Pharisees and the yeast of Herod"** (8.15). The disciples suppose that in mentioning yeast Jesus is talking about them having no bread again. Jesus reviews all that has happened.

"Do you still not perceive or understand?" he asks. This question reaches back to the parable of the sower and echoes God's words to Isaiah (6.9-10). **"Are your hearts hardened? Do you have eyes, and fail to see? Do you have ears, and fail to hear? And do you not remember? When I broke the five loaves for five thousand, how many baskets full of broken pieces did you collect? The disciples answer, 'Twelve.' And the seven for the four thousand, how many baskets full of broken pieces did you collect? The disciples answer, 'Seven.' Then he said to them, 'Do you not yet understand'"** (8.17-21)?

The gospel leaves the disciples and the readers with this unanswered question, one of the gospel writer's silent thresholds where we readers can express our faith. These two feeding miracles are clearly eucharistic. The first provides enough for the twelve tribes of Israel. The second provides seven baskets of leftovers, a number that symbolizes perfection for Gentiles, enough leftovers for all Gentiles. These two feeding miracles reflect on the miracle of eucharist at the heart of building communities of faith. In the second feeding miracle Jesus deliberately takes his mission to Gentiles and includes them. The Syrophoenician woman claims the first crumbs for the Gentile peoples.

The two feeding miracles also celebrate the abundance of creation. Jesus insists on feeding everyone. A little food proves more than enough for all. The stories challenge our communities of faith to do all we can to feed all. **"You give them something to eat,"** Jesus says to his disciples (6.37). In social action as in this eucharistic miracle what seems like a little can multiply.

1 How do you respond to Jesus' question, "Do you understand?" What do the feeding miracles express for you? What do you understand in the baskets of leftovers?

2 What dramatic effects do you see in having the long passage on what is clean and unclean back to back with the story of the Syrophoenician woman?

3 Compare Mark's story of the Syrophoenician woman (7.24-30) and Matthew's (15.21-28).

4 What significance do you see in the four suppliants being the only ones in the gospel who tell Jesus' secret? Whose witness has fueled your faith?

CHAPTER 7

From Blurry Vision to Full Sight
Mark 8.22-10.52

READ MARK 8.22-10.52

Chapter eight marks the halfway point in Mark's gospel, where it turns toward the mystery of Jesus as a suffering messiah. The healing of a blind man in Galilee begins this section; the healing of blind Bartimaeus in Jericho near Jerusalem ends the section; Jesus' journey to Jerusalem unifies the whole. The journey is not merely from Galilee to Jerusalem but from the disciples' blurry sight of who Jesus is to full vision of and insight into him as the suffering messiah. Peter, James, and John have special scenes with Jesus—Peter reacting to Jesus' first passion prediction, James and John seeking status in Jesus' kingdom, all three witnessing Jesus in transfigured glory. This section includes sayings and encounters with people on the journey, giving it a loose form that the three passion predictions move forward and the second sight-giving miracle ends.

The gospel lavishes detail on the healing of the blind man that begins this story strand. The setting is Bethsaida. Jesus takes the man by the hand and leads him out of the village, puts saliva on his eyes, and lays hands on him. When Jesus asks the man if he can see, the man says, **"I can see people but they look like trees, walking"** (8.24). Jesus lays hands on him a second time and looks at him intently. Then the man can see clearly. Jesus sends him to his house and directs him not to go back to the village—not to spread what happened, to keep the secret. This miracle in two stages foreshadows the journey the disciples make from a blurry vision of who Jesus is to full insight in the light of his death and resurrection. At this halfway point in Jesus' ministry, the disciples have seen him preach, heal, cast out unclean spirits, and forgive sins—actions that convince them he is the messiah.

"WHO DO YOU SAY THAT I AM?"
MARK 8.27-9.1

Three short scenes turn the gospel narrative toward to Jerusalem. **"Who do people say that I am?"** Jesus asks his disciples as they visit villages around Caesarea Philippi. The disciples report what the opening verses of Mark's gospel suggest; Jesus is a prophet. Some people say Jesus is **"John the Baptist; others Elijah or one of the prophets"** (8.28). Then Jesus asks the turning point question in the gospel, **"Who do you say that I am"** (8.29)? Peter answers, presumably for the group, **"You are the messiah."** Jesus orders the disciples not to tell anyone about him, to keep his messianic identity secret.

Back to back with this key dialogue, Jesus begins to teach his disciples that he must undergo suffering and rejection, be killed, and on the third day rise again. Peter takes Jesus aside and rebukes him; Jesus retorts, **"Get behind me Satan! For you are setting your mind not on divine things, but on human things"** (8.33). The back-to-back dialogues belong together—Peter's profession of faith and his rebuke. The disciples have a blurry, popular vision of Jesus as messiah.

The passion prediction anticipates what actually happens to Jesus; the disciples can't take it in. A suffering messiah seems a contradiction in terms. The messiah is to be a great king who establishes a kingdom of peace and glory. The three predictions in this section mark steps in the journey to Jerusalem and remind us that the gospel writer knows Jesus' whole story even though at this point the disciples who become apostles don't.

After Jesus' passion prediction, the gospel writer attaches several sayings for later followers. **"Those who want to become my followers, let them deny themselves and take up their cross and follow me"** (8.34). These sayings apply the journey theme to every Christian's life. The sayings invite us into the Christian paradox inherent in Jesus' death and resurrection: those who lose their lives for Jesus' sake or the sake of the gospel will save their lives. Those who give their lives will find their lives.

TRANSFIGURATION
MARK 9.2-8

Mark's narrative follows Jesus' unsettling prediction that he will suffer and die with a transfigured vision of who he is. Jesus takes Peter, James, and John up a high mountain where they see him in dazzling white clothes, talking with Moses and Elijah. This enlightening vision breaks through to Jesus' resurrection and places him among Israel's greatest prophets. Jesus shines with divine presence as Moses did. In talking with God face to face on Mt. Horeb, Moses became so radiant that he had to wear a veil when talking to the people. The presence of God transfigures him. Elijah sought God on the same mountain and found God present no longer in storms and lightning but in the utter silence of interior consciousness. God takes Elijah into the heavens in the fiery chariot of divine presence.

The cloud that spoke at Jesus' baptism speaks again in the transfiguration vision. The cloud image for God originates in the exodus. God leads the people through the wilderness as a cloud by day and column of fire by night. In the transfiguration scene the voice from heaven repeats the same words as at Jesus' baptism, **"This is my son, my beloved."** This time the voice adds, **"Listen to him"** (9.7). What the disciples will learn in listening to Jesus is his teaching that he will suffer, die, and be raised up on the third day. The disciples don't comprehend or anticipate what will happen. This paradox is beyond their imagining.

As the four come down the mountain, Jesus says not to tell what they have seen. This time Jesus identifies when the disciples should begin to tell his whole story. **"Tell no one what you have seen until the Son of Man has risen from the dead"** (9.9). Their ensuing conversation demonstrates their incomprehension. The disciples begin to talk about what resurrection from the dead could mean. Then they ask Jesus about why the scribes say Elijah must return before the messiah. Jesus agrees with the scribes Elijah will come first and declares, **"I tell you Elijah has come"** (9.13). The three disciples say nothing, their silence inviting readers to make connections for them. The reader or hearer of the narrative knows Jesus is talking about John the Baptist, but Peter, James, and John have only blurry vision before Jesus' death and resurrection. The audience for whom Mark writes knows how Peter, James, John, and the other disciples give their lives to spread the gospel message after the resurrection. The audience in A.D. 70 doesn't know how little they comprehended beforehand during Jesus' ministry. The gospel writer wants his audience to see themselves in these first disciples.

ENCOUNTERS ON THE JOURNEY
MARK.9.14-29

A miracle follows the transfiguration scene. The gospels include many miracle stories. As a literary form the miracle story has a simple form:

1. A suppliant approaches Jesus with a need.
2. Jesus heals the person.
3. Witnesses react, usually with amazement, sometimes with criticism.
4. Jesus sends the suppliants on their way.

Because miracle stories have such a simple form, they serve as a vehicle for the early preachers and Christian communities to reflect on questions that arise in their lives. In the case of Jesus' healing an epileptic boy, the miracle story emphasizes the importance of prayer in healing. When Peter, James, John, and Jesus rejoin the other disciples, a crowd has gathered around them. A father has pleaded with them to help his son who has seizures. The disciples cannot help him. When Jesus arrives, he urges the father to believe. Like Jairus, the father cries out, **"I believe; help my unbelief"** (9.24). Jesus takes the boy by the hand as he took Peter's mother-in-law and lifts him up. The disciples ask why they couldn't cast out this spirit. Jesus explains, **"This kind can come out only through prayer"** (9.29).

Geographically Jesus passes on though Galilee, going south toward Jerusalem; theologically he keeps his presence secret so he can teach his disciples. For a second time Jesus predicts his suffering. **"The Son of Man is to be betrayed into human hands, and they will kill him, and three days after being killed he will rise again"** (9.31). The disciples not only don't understand but they are even afraid to question Jesus. Instead as they walk along, they start arguing about who is greatest. Jesus explains, **"Whoever wants to be first must be the last of all and the servant of all"** (9.35).

Jesus continues teaching and traveling. The gospel writer tucks into the narrative miracles, sayings, and encounters. John asks if the disciples should stop a man casting out demons in Jesus' name. Jesus says no, **"Whoever is not against us is for us"** (9.40). A Pharisee asks if divorce is lawful. What does Moses command? **"What God has joined together, let no one separate,"** Jesus quotes from Genesis (10.9). He treats husbands and wives equally, teaching that if either divorces the other and remarries, it is adultery. The disciples try to keep little kids from bothering Jesus. Jesus stops them. **"Whoever does not receive the kingdom of God as a little child will never enter it,"** Jesus says and takes the children in his arms and blesses them (10.15-16). A rich young man asks how to inherit eternal life. He has kept the commandments all his life. **"Go, sell what you own, and give the money to the poor,**

and you will have treasure in heaven; then come, follow me," Jesus suggests (10.21). The young man goes away sad rather than sell his possession. More sayings about wealth follow. Peter brings up the fact the disciples have left everything to follow Jesus. Jesus makes a powerful promise, **"There is no one who has left house or brothers or sisters or mother or father or children or fields for my sake or the sake of the good news who will not receive a hundredfold in this age—houses, brothers, sisters, mothers and children and fields, with persecutions—and in the age to come eternal life"** (10.29-30).

WHEN WILL JESUS' DISCIPLES GET IT?
MARK 10.32-45

As Jesus continues his journey to Jerusalem, he walks ahead of his disciples like a shepherd leading sheep. The disciples feel afraid and amazed. Fear and awe seem contradictory feelings, but according to scholars of comparative religions such as Rudolf Otto, people typically experience the presence of God as attractive and fascinating but at the same time terrifying and awesome. In Mark's gospel, Jesus' disciples and suppliants frequently move from fear for their lives to heightened awe, creating thresholds of faith in the narrative for readers.

Jesus makes his third passion prediction by taking the twelve apart for a special session. The whole company of Jesus' disciples remains uncomprehending as James and John demonstrate.

When James and John ask to sit at Jesus' right and left in his kingdom, we readers sympathize with Jesus as a teacher. He has three times taught that he will suffer in Jerusalem. His disciples as characters in the narrative before Jesus' death and resurrection can't imagine this outcome. In asking to be his right and left-hand men, James and John envision themselves in the glory of his kingdom. Their request demonstrates a willingness to commit wholeheartedly to his work.

Jesus thickens the plot with a challenge that anticipates a pre- and post-Easter future. In the immediate future, Jesus judges correctly that these two bewildered and bedazzled disciples don't know what they are asking. They don't imagine falling asleep as he prays in the garden after the last supper. They don't imagine fleeing when officials arrest him. They should answer no when Jesus asks, **"Are you able to drink the cup that I drink or be baptized with the baptism that I am baptized with"** (10.38)? Mark's gospel wants its audience to see these well-known disciples in their pre-Easter confusion, but at the same time to hear in their rash insistence their future as post-Easter apostles who commit their lives to Jesus' good news. The cup is death, martyrdom. The cup Jesus drinks at the last supper pledges his lifeblood as a new covenant.

Blood symbolizes life. In their encounter with God in the wilderness Moses and the people that become Israel seal their agreement to live the ten commandments with blood. Moses sprinkles the blood of an animal on an altar to God and on the people (Exodus 24.6-8). This action is a way of swearing with their lives to keep the law—may my blood be spilled if I don't keep the agreement. Christians understand Jesus' actions at the last supper as making a new covenant in his lifeblood, which he pours out in living his mission unto death.

James and John insist they can drink the same cup of martyrdom. James does. He becomes the leader of the Jerusalem community and is put to death in A.D. 55. John's gospel remembers John standing with Mary at Jesus' cross; tradition remembers John caring for Mary and living a long life dedicated to spreading the gospel. So the two brothers are ultimately right. They can drink the cup. They do give their lives to the gospel and to Jesus' mission. Mark's audience in 70 A.D. that lives in fear after the destruction of the temple and martyrdom of Peter and Paul can recognize they are where James and John were to begin.

Attached to this story are sayings that teach service rather than status as the ideal of the Christian community. **"Whoever wishes to become great must be slave of all"** (10.44). Perhaps more disciples than James and John have to work through their ambitions.

THE MODEL DISCIPLE
MARK 10.46-52

The long journey to Jerusalem and to insight into who Jesus is climaxes with the healing of a blind beggar named Bartimaeus, who sits along the road near Jericho, east of Jerusalem 30 miles. Bartimaeus shouts out a full confession of faith when he hears Jesus is passing by. **"Jesus, Son of David, have mercy on me"** (10.47). Son of David is a title for the king, the messiah. Twice Bartimaeus shouts this out. He won't be quieted. Bartimaeus wants to see; in fact, his faith does see. Jesus affirms, **"Go, your faith has made you well"** (10.52). In this healing Jesus makes another disciple. Bartimaeus follows Jesus on his way.

Mark's gospel characterizes the journey that Jesus leads to Jerusalem not only as Jesus' journey toward suffering but his disciples' journey toward deeper faith. Jesus is not the messiah Peter thinks he is. Jesus is not the king James and John seek to serve. Jesus is a prophet like Moses and Elijah in Israel's history, clothed in both glory and suffering. Jesus is the itinerant preacher a rich, young man turns away from and a blind beggar follows.

1   What effect does the gospel narrative gain by putting Peter's profession of faith (8.27-30) and Jesus' first passion prediction (8.31-33) back to back?

2   How do Jesus' repeated predictions of his suffering, death, and resurrection function for the disciples who follow him to Jerusalem? How do the predictions function for you as a gospel reader today?

3   What insight about who Jesus is do you gain from the transfiguration scene, which places Jesus with Israel's greatest prophets? How is Jesus like Elijah and Moses?

4   Contrast the healings of blind men that begin and end this section. What does Bartimaeus (10.46-52) see about Jesus that the first blind man doesn't (8.22-26)? What do the disciples see and not see at the end of this section?

CHAPTER 8

"Not the Season for Figs"

Mark 11.1-12.44

READ MARK 11.1-12.44

Every city and village has its central gathering place, every capitol its plaza for protests. In Jerusalem the temple and its courts provide this place. Jesus gravitates to the temple once he enters Jerusalem, the opening scene of this section of the gospel. The temple stands atop Jerusalem's highest hill with large open courts surrounding it and a colonnade for sellers at its perimeters. At this place where Jews of Jesus' time ascend to celebrate feasts and offer prayers and sacrifices, Jesus engages the controversial questions of his day with representatives of various religious groups—the chief priests of the temple, scribes, Pharisees, Herodians, and Sadducees. Typically these controversy stories involve dialogue rather than action. The stories reflect the religious crosswinds in which Jesus taught and early Christians lived his teachings.

This section begins with Jesus' entry into Jerusalem, a scene familiar from Palm Sunday. Jesus sends two disciples ahead to Jerusalem as he arrives a couple of miles east at the village of Bethany. The account focuses for seven verses on the colt Jesus rides into the city, which gives the animal surprising emphasis. Jesus tells the disciples to bring to him a colt they will find tied in the village. It has never been ridden. If anyone objects, Jesus directs, **"Just say this, 'The Lord needs it and will send it back immediately'"** (11.3). The disciples proceed exactly as Jesus has directed, proving him a knowledgeable leader and the colt a significant symbol.

This scene deliberately contrasts Jesus' entry riding a colt with a warrior's triumphal and intimidating entry astride a great steed with a phalanx of soldiers behind. Jesus comes in peace rather than military power. The people welcome him by laying their cloaks and palm branches on the road. The words the crowd shouts recognize Jesus is the messiah, **"Hosanna! Blessed is the one who comes in the name of the Holy One. Blessed is the coming kingdom of our ancestor David. Hosanna in highest heaven"** (11.9-10).

CLEANSING THE TEMPLE
MARK 11.12-26

Jesus' first action after entering Jerusalem is cleansing the temple, the meaty middle of one of Mark's literary sandwiches. The slices of story that surround the cleansing feature a fig tree. On his way to the temple the day after entering Jerusalem, Jesus sees a fig tree, feels hungry, and goes to it in search of figs to eat. **"When he came to it, he found nothing but leaves, for it was not the season for figs"** (11.13). This fig tree symbolizes the temple, lots of showy leaves, no fruit.

Mark's gospel provides clear details about Jesus' actions in the temple. He drives out those selling and buying; he overturns the tables of the money changers and the seats of the dove sellers. The account puts an interpretative verse in Jesus' mouth. He quotes Isaiah (56.7), **"Is it not written, 'My house shall be called a house of prayer for all the nations?' But you have made it a den of robbers?"** (11.17). Jesus' actions cause a stir. The officials look for a way to kill him. The crowds find his teaching spellbinding.

The next day the disciples notice the fig tree has withered to its roots. From the viewpoint of the gospel writer in A.D. 70, the temple has dried up as a source of spiritual community. Its destruction leaves not one stone upon another and confirms Jesus' prophetic, cleansing actions. Jesus finds the tree without fruit in his lifetime; at the writing of the gospel, the temple is gone, withered.

Many of Jesus' teachings take the form of sayings and parables. The gospel writer attaches these sayings where their themes fit the narrative action. Since Jesus cleanses the temple to restore it as a place of prayer, the gospel attaches a saying on prayer to the disciples' discovery of the withered fig tree. **"If you say to this mountain, 'Be taken up and thrown into the sea, and if you do not doubt in your heart, but believe that what you say will come to pass, it will be done for you. So I tell you, whatever you ask for in prayer, believe that you have received it, and it will be yours"** (11.23-24). A second short saying also finds a home here. It emphasizes that prayer must include forgiving others so our Father in heaven can forgive us. The first gospel includes only this short part of the prayer Christians today call the Our Father or the Lord's Prayer.

CONTROVERSIES
MARK 11.27-12.44

Predictably the temple authorities, including chief priests, scribes, and elders, confront Jesus after he upsets temple commerce. They want to know, **"By whose authority are you doing these things?"** (11.28). Jesus responds with a question that shows the officials have read the latest political polls. Jesus asks if they consider the baptism of John to come from heaven or from human origin. The officials know the crowds that Jesus holds spellbound also consider the Baptist a prophet from God. They don't answer. Jesus confronts them indirectly with the parable of the tenants. Their question about by whose authority Jesus acts looms over these debates for readers and hearers to decide.

The parable of the tenants riffs on the 8th century prophet Isaiah's song of the vineyard that describes the house of Israel as the vineyard of God (Isaiah 5.1-7). Both the prophet and parable describe the labor involved in planting a vineyard and the expectation the work builds for a fruitful harvest. The parable as we receive it in the gospel has become a post-Easter allegory of Jesus' life. After the tenants beat and kill the owner's slave, the owner sends a beloved son to collect the harvest. Similiarly, the voice at Jesus' baptism and at his transfiguration calls Jesus "beloved Son." With this allegory the parable becomes theology; early Christians use the Hebrew scriptures to articulate who Jesus is and to interpret the destruction of the temple.

In the parable the owner destroys the tenants and gives the vineyard to others. In history the destruction of the temple ends the worship its priests led and the sacrifices they offered. Oral tradition also attaches to this parable a short passage from Psalm 118 that interprets the whole parable. Jesus is the stone the builders rejected that has become the cornerstone, the one around whom a new community of faith has gathered. The officials catch on that the parable is about them; they leave but send others to question Jesus on controversial topics.

The Herodians, who accept and support the Roman-appointed king Herod, attempt to trap Jesus with a question about paying taxes. **"Is it lawful to pay taxes to the emperor or not?"** Jesus tricks them instead when he notices that they already have in hand the Roman coins for paying taxes. The coins offended Jews because they had the emperor's image on them. The Herodians's question provides a setting for Jesus' teaching, **"Give to the emperor the things that are the emperor's and to God the things that are God's"** (12.17). Jesus' teaching amazes the questioners just as his healings amazed witnesses in Galilee. Repeatedly in Mark's gospel the narrative moves witnesses to amazement, to the threshold of faith.

The Sadducees confront Jesus next. Among the Jewish groups of Jesus' time, they are the most conservative. They believe only in the first five books of the law (Genesis, Exodus, Leviticus, Numbers, and Deuteronomy), not any oral precedents as the Pharisees do. They are like strict constructionists in regard to the U.S. Constitution today. The Sadducees don't believe in resurrection. They present a case that mocks this belief. If a man dies and his brother marries his wife and this happens down the family, so seven brothers have married the same wife, whose wife will she be in the resurrection of the dead?

Jesus responds that people don't marry in heaven. Then he shows he knows Israel's scriptures as he argues for resurrection of the dead from the book of Exodus, one of the books of Torah that the Sadducees accept. Jesus argues that when God speaks to Moses, God remembers Israel's earlier ancestors, saying, **"I am the God of Abraham, the God of Isaac, and the God of Jacob."** Jesus concludes, **"God is God not of the dead but of the living"** (12.27).

Jesus' arguments impress a scribe who is observing his teaching. The scribe asks the basic question, "Which commandment is first of all?" Jesus answers with his people's most basic prayer, called the *Shema* (*Sheeh-mah*) after its first word in Hebrew: **"Hear, O Israel, the Lord our God is one; you shall love the Lord with all your heart, and with all your soul, and with all your strength"** (Deuteronomy 6.4-5). Jesus adds a second commandment, **"You shall love your neighbor as yourself"** (Leviticus 19.18). The scribe agrees God is one and agrees love of neighbor is a more important way to worship God than sacrifices. Jesus affirms the scribe is not far from the kingdom. This positive outcome ends the controversies.

The narrative tucks in a three-verse teaching that depends on word play. How can the scribes say that the messiah is the son of David when in the first verse of Psalm 110 King David calls God Lord? The messiah is God's Son, not the king's son. This argument delights the crowd.

In back to back short scenes the narrative has Jesus offer summary criticism of the scribes and hold up a model of religious authenticity. He criticizes scribes who wear long robes and expect places and greetings of honor but devour the resources of widows, the persons with the least in the society of the time.

Jesus points to a widow as an ideal faithful Israelite in contrast to the scribes and other officials. This woman contributes to the temple treasury everything she has to live. What is worthy of praise is not the size of the gift or the place that receives the gift. The gift deserves praise because it is wholehearted. The pennies express more than a duty; they express love of God, a relationship between the widow and the One who gives her life and on whom she depends for life. Her example stands contrary to the wealthy who give for show or give out of so much abundance they don't feel the gift. Like Bartimaeus, this nameless widow offers a model of whole-hearted response to God, uninfluenced by shifting religious winds.

1 How are the controversies Jesus faces like those Christians face today?

2 What questions would you ask Jesus about divorce today?

3 How does the good scribe change your assumptions about who the scribes and Pharisees are?

4 How is the story of the widow's temple offering a fitting close to Mark 11-12?

5 Chapters 11 and 12 take place in the temple courtyard just a few days before Jesus' passion. How are these scenes like controversies among Christians today?

JERUSALEM IN JESUS' TIME

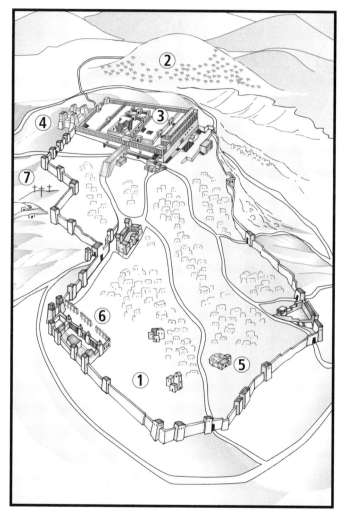

1 Upper Room

2 Mount of Olives

3 Temple

4 Antonia Fortress

5 High Priest's House

6 Pilate's Quarters

7 Golgotha

CHAPTER 9

"Not One Stone Upon Another"

Mark 13.1-37

READ MARK 13.1-37.

In all three synoptic gospels Jesus admires the great Second Temple King Herod built and prophesies its end. **"There will not be left here one stone upon another"** (13.2). The temple stood for 40 years after Jesus' lifetime. In A.D. 66, a Jewish rebellion for independence from Rome began. Four years later after a long siege of the city, Roman soldiers destroyed Jerusalem, its walls, and the temple on its highest hill.

Chapter 13 in Mark's gospel stands out from the rest of the narrative. This chapter is a mini apocalypse. The last book of the New Testament, Revelations, is a much longer apocalypse. Apocalyptic is a highly symbolic literary genre that uses visions, codes, and symbols to express oppressed people's hope that good will triumph over evil. In apocalyptic writing the world is falling apart. Even the usually stable sun, moon, and stars fall from the sky; famines, plagues, and wars run rampant. It's a scary way to give hope.

Contemporary films such as *Lord of the Rings, Star Wars,* and the *Harry Potter* series are like apocalyptic, creating mythic battles between good and evil in imaginary worlds. Like apocalyptic writing, the science fiction genre affirms good will triumph over the dark side.

The spirituals that developed among African Americans during slavery also have an apocalyptic flavor with codes and symbols that express hope oppression will end. A chariot will swing low and carry a slave home. Moses will again set people free. In the song "Steal Away," an owner hears slaves seeking comfort in Jesus their Savior. A slave hears the signal that the coast is clear to escape.

An apocalyptic writer seeks to answer the questions: How much longer will people suffer? How long before God saves us from our enemies? Apocalyptic writing offers a time table. For example, the prophet Daniel describes a vision of four beasts—a lion with eagle wings, a devouring bear, a leopard with four heads and bird wings, and a beast with iron teeth and ten horns. These beasts symbolize the nations that had conquered Israel—the Assyrians, the Babylonians, the Persians, the Greeks. Then the prophet sees another vision—**"the Ancient One coming to destroy the four beasts and one like a human coming on clouds to rule with justice"** (Daniel 7.1-14). Early Christians see Jesus in this vision and use "Son of Man" as a title for him.

In 44 B.C., the Romans become the fifth conquerors to rule Palestine and absorb the country into its empire. It is the Roman Tenth Legion that destroys the temple in A.D. 70 after a long siege of the city of Jerusalem. Today the Blue Mosque stands on the 30-acre plaza that Herod built.

Jews worship at the Western Wall, all that is left of the temple, the western retaining wall of the temple mount. A great engineer and builder, Herod expanded the temple courts and refurbished the 500-year-old building.

Mark's little apocalypse is a collection of apocalyptic sayings that offer different points of view about when the end will be. The chapter begins as Jesus and his disciples leave the temple where he has been teaching. One exclaims about the temple's beauty—**"What stones, and what a building!"** In response Jesus prophesies, **"There will be not one stone left upon another"** (13.2). In A.D. 70, when Mark writes, these words have come true. The temple lies in ruins. This is the verse that places the writing of the gospel in the aftermath of the destruction of the temple. Its destruction ends temple-centered worship, sacrifices, and festive pilgrimages to celebrate Passover and Pentecost.

Peter, Andrew, James, and John leave the temple and go with Jesus to the Mount of Olives, where they sit across a valley from the great temple. The disciples seek a revelation about when the temple will fall. The chapter collects six groups of sayings, each with a different flavor. In the first group of sayings Jesus grants there will be wars, earthquakes, and famines but sees these as labor pains, birthing pains, not the end (13.3-8). In the second group of sayings Jesus warns that his followers will be persecuted but promises the Holy Spirit will speak in them in the hour they face death. **"Those who persevere will be saved"** (13.9-13). In fact, by the time Mark is writing, Peter, James, and Paul have been martyred.

The third group of sayings holds up the "desolating abomination" as the sign to flee the city immediately. For the only time in the narrative the gospel speaks directly to the reader, **"Let the reader understand"** (13.14). The abomination may be the presence of Roman gods dese-crating the temple. The urgency of these sayings may re-flect Christians' experience during the siege of Jerusalem and their flight from the city.

The fourth group of sayings has a classic apocalyptic set-ting. The sun will darken, the stars fall from the sky; then as Daniel prophesied, **"They will see the Son of Man coming on the clouds with great power and glory"** (13.26). With the coming of the Son of Man a time of judgment arrives; he sends out angels to gather the elect from the four winds.

The fifth set of sayings insists the Son of Man will come soon. Just as everyone knows summer is near when a fig tree sprouts leaves, so the catastrophic events around the de-struction of the temple signal the end. **"This generation will not pass away until all these things have taken place. Heaven and earth will pass away, but my words will not"** (13.31).

Chapter 13 concludes with sayings that insist to the con-trary no one knows the day or hour of the end, **"neither the angels in heaven, nor the Son, but only the Father"** (13.32). This sixth group of sayings counsels, **"Be watchful! Be alert! You do not know when the time will come"** (13.33).

Instead of a date for the end of all things, Jesus gives his disciples a parable about an estate owner who goes on a journey, leaves his slaves in charge, and commands the door-keeper to be on the watch. No one knows when the owner will return. The parable includes a timetable. The owner may come in the evening, at midnight, at cockcrow, at dawn.

These times of day anticipate moments in the journey Jesus' disciples make with him during his passion, which begins in the next chapter. In the evening, at midnight, at cockcrow Jesus' disciples fail to watch.

In the evening Peter, James, and John fall asleep when they accompany Jesus to the garden after their Passover meal together. They sleep through the opportunity to be present to a friend in his agonizing hour.

At midnight, Judas leads a crowd to arrest his Teacher. All the other disciples except Peter fear for their lives and flee. Their survival instincts kick in and they split.

Peter follows Jesus to the high priest's house, where a servant girl suggests he is with the Nazarene, but Peter denies even knowing Jesus. A cock crowing wakes Peter up that he has denied his friend. He has boastfully overpromised his loyalty. Mark suspends Peter in tears and regret.

Dawn is the fourth time of day, the hour when Mary Magdalene, Mary the mother of James and Joses, and Salome find Jesus' tomb empty. This is the hour of resurrection, of awakening.

Evening, midnight, cockcrow, and dawn mark stages in the process of maturing faith. This birthing process moves in the disciples from slumber, to fear, to denial, to regret and awakening.

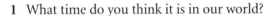

1 What time do you think it is in our world?

2 Where in the birthing process is your faith? Slumbering, wakening, hoping?

3 How powerful for you is the promise of Jesus coming again in glory? How, if at all, does this promise affect your spirituality?

4 How do you stay awake spiritually?

CHAPTER 10

"Are you the Son of the Blessed One?"

Mark 14.1-15.47

READ MARK 14.1-15.47.

The opening chapters of Mark's gospel describe Jesus' actions day by day during the first week of his ministry in Galilee. Chapters14-16 describe the events of Jesus' final days in Jerusalem. Mark writes in an everyday Greek, in which a conjunction begins each sentence. This creates a narrative that rolls out in simple, straightforward sentences linked "and then, and then." The tragic action marches relentlessly forward.

For all the simplicity of its sentences, the gospel laces the passion narrative with biting, theological irony. As characters in the narrative, Jesus' disciples experience the unfolding events without knowing how they will turn out. Of the men who follow Jesus from Galilee, one betrays him and all but Peter desert him. Peter denies knowing him. The religious officials judge Jesus a serious threat to their leadership among the people. The Roman governor has the power to protect an innocent man but goes with the crowd. Roman soldiers mock Jesus as king with a crown of thorns. Bystanders want Jesus to prove he is the messiah by coming down from the cross. Only three women followers stand with Jesus at his crucifixion and two help bury his body. The passion narrative conveys the deep theological irony that a messiah who suffers and dies for his healing and teaching is not the messiah either disciples or religious officials expected.

In Jerusalem Christians can walk Jesus' last walk, the way of the cross. The Mount of Olives rises across a valley from the temple mount. The steps to the High Priest's house remain. Golgotha remains, a site of Christian veneration within the Church of the Holy Sepulcher. The Romans crucified enemies of the empire outside the ancient city walls where permanent holes in the rocks were ready to hold upright the wooden beams on which they roped or nailed the condemned. The exact place of Jesus' tomb is not certain although the Church of the Holy Sepulcher takes its name from being the site of Jesus' burial and has graves from the first century beneath it.

The practice of making the way of the cross continues not only in Jerusalem but in Catholic churches and along retreat paths, wherever Christians use the Stations of the Cross to visualize, remember, and accompany Jesus in his passion. This devotion helps make the places in the narrative familiar as does hearing the passion during Holy Week liturgies. The passion narrative moves from Simon's house in Bethany two miles outside Jerusalem, to an upper room in the city for the Passover meal, to the Mount of Olives where Jesus prays, to the High Priest's house for Jesus' trial, to Pilate's palace for his condemnation, to Golgotha for the crucifixion, and to the tomb.

THE ANOINTING
MARK 14.1-11

The time in chapter 14 is two days before the Jewish feast of Passover, which celebrates God passing over the homes of the Hebrew slaves marked with the blood of lambs. The blood saves them from the tenth plague, the deaths of first born sons and animals, the plague that convinced Pharaoh to let them go. The killing of the lambs for this feast happens the day before Passover at the temple.

The first 11 verses form a literary sandwich, foreshadowing the plot of the passion. To begin, the chief priests and scribes look for a way to kill Jesus (14.1-2). In the meaty middle scene, a woman prophetically anoints Jesus during a meal at the home of Simon the leper in Bethany (14.3-9). In the second slice of sandwich Judas goes to the chief priests and agrees to betray Jesus (14.10-11). The narrative surrounds the prophetic anointing of Jesus with plots against his life.

Jesus' words as the anointing scene concludes make the woman's prophetic action essential to the gospel. He insists, **"Wherever the good news is proclaimed in the whole world what she has done will be told in memory of her"** (14.9). John's gospel identifies this woman as Mary, the sister of Martha and Lazarus, who live in Bethany. Mark's gospel leaves the woman unnamed but remembers her for breaking open an alabaster jar of costly ointment and pouring the oil on Jesus' head. Israel anointed its kings by pouring oil on their heads. The woman's gesture is a prophetic act that identifies Jesus as the messiah. Her act anticipates what Jesus' resurrection proclaims. He is the messiah, the

Son of God. The woman's action also anticipates the reason the chief priest and Sanhedrin condemn Jesus.

Insultingly, the male guests talk about the woman in her presence without talking to her. They criticize her action without her having voice. Jesus silences their criticism that the ointment should have been sold and the money given to the poor. He affirms the woman's action. **"She has performed a good service for me"** (14.6). Jesus connects her service with his burial. **"She has done what she could; she has anointed my body beforehand for its burial"** (14.8). When the three women take spices to anoint his body three days after his death, they find the tomb empty with no body to anoint. The anointing as the passion begins both identifies Jesus as the messiah and prepares him for burial.

LAST SUPPER
MARK 14.12-25

The passion narrative spends five verses on detailed arrangements for a Passover supper. Jesus sends his disciples to find a man carrying a jar of water who will go to a house where the owner will have a room ready; in fact, these directions play out, making Jesus a trustworthy person to follow. What he says will happen unfolds about everyday matters. At the supper Jesus prophesies that one of his own will betray him, a statement the reader already knows is true. Jesus continues to make prophetic statements that prove true, making him increasingly trustworthy and knowledgeable about his destiny. This post-Easter way of telling the story can make contemporary readers see Jesus living out a preordained, divine script. The hindsight and insight of those who hand on Jesus' story don't take away what Jesus suffered—betrayal, condemnation, torture, execution by crucifixion, and ultimately his final act of entrusting himself forsaken into the hands of God.

The Passover meal takes place in the evening. A new day begins at sunset, so the last supper and Jesus' crucifixion happen on the same day. At the supper Jesus makes prophetic gestures that anticipate and interpret his death on the cross. At this meal Jesus blesses, breaks and shares bread, identifying the bread with his body. **"Take it; this is my body"**(14.22). He blesses and shares a cup of wine, identifying the cup of wine with his lifeblood. **"This is my blood of the covenant, which is poured out for many"**(14.23). Jesus refers to sharing this cup as a new covenant, a new agreement in our relationship with God. Ancient Israel ratified its covenant of the commandments in blood, signifying that the people promised to stand by the agreement with their lives (Exodus 24.1-8). The Christian community that tells Jesus' story understands his actions as making a covenant sealed in his own lifeblood that expresses his willingness to love them unto death. The narrative attaches an apocalyptic saying looking beyond Jesus' death to his resurrection. **"Truly I tell you, I will never again drink of the fruit of the vine until that day when I drink it new in the kingdom of God"** (14.25).

THE READER AS INSIDER
MARK 14.26-51

The gospel writer arranges the whole gospel and the passion narrative itself to lead hearers and readers to the meaning of Jesus' death and resurrection and to call us to faith. Jesus anticipates what will happen to him. At supper Jesus prophesies that one of his own will betray him. After supper at the Mount of Olives Jesus quotes an Old Testament prophesy, **"You will all become deserters; for it is written, 'I will strike the shepherd and the sheep will be scattered.' But after I am raised up, I will go before you to Galilee** (14.27-28). Jesus also insists that Peter will deny him three times before cockcrow.

These prophecies set up the hearer of the story as an insider who knows how the plot will unfold. From the first verse the reader knows the claim Mark's gospel makes—Jesus is the messiah. As each prophesy comes true, Jesus becomes an increasingly trustworthy voice until only his promise of being raised up and going before his friends into Galilee remains unfulfilled, the ultimate threshold of faith.

The messianic secret and the three passion predictions also make readers and hearers insiders. We know the leper, the deaf man, the blind man were not to tell that Jesus healed them but told anyway. We know that Jesus warns Peter to tell no one his profession that **"You are the messiah"** (8.29). We know that Peter, James, and John witness the raising up of Jairus's daughter, but never tell in the gospel what happened. We learn with Peter, James, and John after the transfiguration when the time to tell will arrive—after Jesus has risen from the dead (9.9). We know on the eve of Jesus' passion that one disciple will betray him, all the disciples will scatter, and Peter will deny him. Ironically, Peter and all the disciples with him insist they will stand with Jesus to the end.

At this point the narrative Jesus takes Peter, James, and John with him to a garden on the Mount of Olives to pray. Jesus asks for the support they have just pledged. **"I am deeply grieved, even to death; remain here and stay awake"** (14.34). Each of the three times Jesus goes aside to pray the three fall asleep. It is night and they don't keep watch. They are asleep to Jesus' agony and the unfolding drama.

Unlike the three disciples, the omniscient narrator stays awake and creates Jesus' interior consciousness at prayer. At his most human in this prayer Jesus agonizes over the possibility of death. He has pledged his lifeblood in the cup of the covenant at the last supper but in prayer dreads martyrdom. **"Abba, Father, for you all things are possible, remove this cup from me; yet, not what I want but what you want"** (14.36). The three times Jesus wakes up his disciples intensifies their failure to support him and his aloneness at this hour. The hour of Jesus' passion comes at the end of his prayer. **"My betrayer is at hand,"** he says as he awakens the three sleepers (14.42).

Judas's kiss fulfills Jesus' prophecy that one of his own will betray him. Jesus challenges why the guards and crowd with Judas have come with swords and clubs to arrest him as if he were a bandit when they could have arrested him any day in the temple courtyards as he taught. At this point Jesus says simply, **"Let the scriptures be fulfilled"** (14.49). His prophesies anticipate the events about to unfold. Immediately his followers flee and fulfill his prophesy that the sheep will scatter. Jesus speaks again only to answer the accusations of the high priest and governor and in the words of Psalm 22 on the cross.

THE TRIAL
MARK 14.53-72

Judas and the crowd take Jesus to the home of the high priest for trial before the religious council. Artfully the narrative creates an inside and outside scene during Jesus' trial. Peter follows Jesus to the high priest's house. The narrative places Peter outside in the courtyard, sitting with the guards, warming himself at their fire (14.54). Inside the house the trial begins. Witnesses testify against Jesus that he said, **"I will destroy this temple that is made with hands and in three days I will build another, not made with hands"** (14.58). The witnesses don't agree. Jesus keeps silent. The frustrated high priest finally asks the ultimate question, **"Are you the Son of the Blessed One?"** Jesus breaks his silence and answers, **"I am."** These words translate the name of God in the Old Testament—*I am who am.* Jesus acknowledges he is the messiah (14.62). His silence except for these words enhances their meaning. The gospel writer adds a reference to the prophet Daniel's vision, **"You will see the Son of Man seated at the right hand of the Power, and "coming with the clouds of heaven'"** (14.62).

The high priest accuses Jesus of blasphemy and tears his clothes. The council condemns Jesus. People spit on him. The guards beat him. All this happens inside the high priest's house.

Meanwhile outside in the courtyard a serving girl spots Peter. **"You were with Jesus, the man from Nazareth,"** she says (14.67). He denies it, moves to a new spot in the courtyard, and hears a cockcrow. The serving girl spots Peter a second time and insists, **"This man is one of them"** (14.69). Peter again denies it. Then a bystander takes up the accusation, **"Certainly, you are one of them, for you are a Galilean"** (14.70). This time Peter swears no, **"I do not know the man you are talking about"** (14.71). A cock crows again, reminding Peter of Jesus' prophesy. Peter breaks down and the narrative leaves him weeping in profound regret. With the inside and outside scenes the narrative creates the effect that Jesus' affirmation he is the messiah and Peter's denial happen simultaneously.

CRUCIFIXION
MARK 15

In the morning the chief priests, elders, scribes, and whole council agree to hand Jesus over to Pilate, the Roman governor who can execute a death penalty. Pilate asks essentially the same question as the high priest, **"Are you the king of the Jews?"** Jesus answers only, **"You say so"** (15.2). His terse answer underscores the charge against him—his claim to be the messiah. His silence beyond these words amazes Pilate, his unwillingness to defend himself. Pilate sees the Jewish officials acting out of jealousy in handing Jesus over to him and sees a way out for himself in giving the crowd a chance to release Jesus rather than the insurrectionist Barrabas on the occasion of Passover. But Jesus' opponents have stirred up the crowd and they prefer Barrabas. Pilate asks, **"What should I do with the man you call King of the Jews?"** The crowd yells, **"Crucify him"** (15.13). Pilate satisfies the crowd.

In Mark's gospel Jesus endures flogging, mocking, and crucifixion without speaking. The Roman soldiers clothe him in purple, twist thorns into a crown for his head, and salute him as "King of the Jews." They hit his head with a reed, spit on him, and kneel in mocking homage. They lead Jesus out of the city to crucify him. They press Simon of Cyrene to carry Jesus' cross. The soldiers crucify Jesus at nine in the morning. The charge against him reads, "The King of the Jews," the third time the narrative identifies this messianic title with Jesus' offense.

Passersby taunt Jesus. **"Let the messiah, the king of Israel, come down from the cross now so that we can see and believe"** (14.32). Jesus doesn't speak. At noon darkness fills the land until three when Jesus prays Psalm 22, **"My God, my God, why have you forsaken me?"** We feel desolation in the words. Crucifixion kills through asphyxiation. The condemned on the cross must lift themselves up to breathe. They hang by the arms but have a foot rest from which they can push themselves up with their legs. This is a tortuous position in which people can survive in public shame and scorn for some time. When bystanders hear Jesus' prayer, they think he is calling for the prophet Elijah. A centurion near the cross sees Jesus has taken his last breath and says, **"Truly this man was God's Son"** (15.39). These words reiterate the claims in the first verse of Mark's gospel. Jesus is the Christ, the Son of God. Christians hear in the centurion's words a confession of faith and an affirmation of their own faith. The centurion's words could be ironic in the same tone as the ridicule of the bystanders.

WOMEN WITNESSES
MARK 15.40-47

At this point the narrative moves back from the moment of Jesus' death on the cross and brings Jesus' women followers into the scene. Mary Magdalene, Mary the mother of James the younger and Joses, and Salome look on the scene at a distance. Not all of Jesus' disciples fled at his arrest.

These women have the credentials of disciples. They have followed Jesus, served him, and come up with him to Jerusalem (15.41). They are invisible until this point in the narrative when they witness Jesus' crucifixion and burial. Mary Magdalene and Mary the mother of Joses accompany a man named Joseph to the tomb where they lay Jesus' body and roll a stone into the door of the tomb (15.46).

These women of Galilee follow Jesus farther than all others in the gospel. They witness the crucifixion and see where Jesus is buried. They stand with someone they love to the end and help bury the body.

1   Why must the account of the woman anointing Jesus be told in her memory wherever the good news is told? How do we respond to Jesus' request that we tell her story?

2   What do his prophetic statements contribute to how you see Jesus in his passion? What does his silence contribute?

3   Why does the passion narrative characterize Jesus' male disciples so negatively?

4   What is the purpose of bringing in the women disciples after Jesus has died?

5   What most touches and inspires you in the passion narrative?

CHAPTER 11

The Ultimate Threshold of Faith: the Empty Tomb

Mark 16.1-8

READ MARK 16.1-8.

In Chapter 16 the hour arrives to tell the good news about Jesus, the secret he directed Peter, James, and John not to tell until now. The third day to which Jesus' three passion predictions point is here. **"The Son of Man must undergo great suffering, and be rejected by the elders, the chief priests, and the scribes, and be killed, and after three days rise again"** (8.31; also 9.31; 10.34). The time is dawn. The servants' hours of failed attention at their master's door have passed—the disciples' repeated snoozing during Jesus' prayer in the evening, their flight at his midnight arrest, and Peter's regret at cockcrow. The hour of waking is here. The narrative builds toward this moment when the three women disciples who witnessed Jesus' crucifixion and burial—Mary Magdalene, Mary the mother of James and Joses, and Salome—head for the tomb to anoint Jesus' body properly with spices they have bought. **"And very early on the first day of the week, when the sun had risen, they went to the tomb"** (16.2).

The passion narrative begins and ends with an anointing. The woman who lavished expensive ointment on Jesus' head both anointed him messiah as Israel anointed its kings and prepared his body beforehand for burial. The women who go to the tomb find no body to anoint. Like the sea-crossing story strand, the feeding strand, and the stories and teachings within the sight-giving miracle, the passion narrative has oral parenthesis—the two anointings, the first anticipating what the women cannot complete at the empty tomb.

As the women go to the tomb, they worry about how to roll away the stone Joseph moved over the entrance to the tomb. But they find the tomb open, its doorway a threshold or liminal space between death and life, between the foreboding inner tomb and the waking outside world, between fear and faith. The tomb is cave-like with multiple places to put bodies and space enough for the three to enter. In Mark's gospel what the women find in the tomb is neither the body of the crucified Jesus nor the risen Jesus himself. Unexpectedly the women find a young man in a white robe inside the tomb. **"They were amazed"** (16.5). What fills the tomb is the young man's proclamation of the core of the gospel: **"Do not be amazed,"** he says to the women. **"You seek Jesus of Nazareth, who was crucified. He has risen, he is not here; see the place where they laid him"** (16.6).

The young man commissions the women, **"Go, tell his disciples and Peter that he is going ahead of you to**

Galilee; there you will see him just as he told you" (16.7). The women flee the tomb, **"for terror and amazement had seized them"** (16.8). To be seized is to be taken over, changed. The women are experiencing the numinous feelings that comparative religion scholar Rudolf Otto identifies as typical of the experience of the holy—terror, awe, fear, fascination. Trembling (*tromos* in Greek) shakes their bones. Ecstasy (*ekstasis* in Greek) carries them outside themselves and beyond their deepest hopes. The gospel pictures the women in awe and silence, primal religious feelings. Then in the last six Greek words the gospel suspends the narrative with the women's commission to tell unfulfilled. **"And they said nothing to anyone because they were afraid"** (16.8).

By suspending the women in an unspeakable, numinous silence, the gospel climaxes in an apotheosis, a revelation that has not yet come to words. Once the women speak, this moment of grace and awe will end; words, when they speak them, will describe an experience past rather than present. The narrative preserves the moment and suspends the women deliberately in wordless awe at this threshold where faith begins.

In the first written gospel the disciples of history become characters in story, no longer living and breathing but forever frozen in the significance the author wants readers to see in them. The three women become forever Easter women, who invite new generations of hearers to profess the faith the young man in the white robe speaks in the tomb. Their role as characters is to invite hearers to step across the threshold of faith, into the death and resurrection of Jesus, into the baptism font.

The omniscient narrator brings Mary Magdalene, Mary the mother of James and Joses, and Salome into the gospel story only after Jesus has died on the cross and the centurion has echoed the words of its first verse, **"Truly, this man is the Son of God"** (15.39). By witnessing Jesus' death and burial and finding his tomb empty, they write an implicit eyewitness signature to the whole narrative. The suspended ending of the narrative disengages us hearers and readers from the story world of the narrative. The women's silence functions like Jesus' provocative silence before the high priest and Pilate and his silent acceptance of the taunts of passersby on the cross. It creates emptiness in which meaning resonates.

When the women fall silent, we hearers have already heard in the written gospel the story they don't tell. The truth claims of the narrative echo in our minds and can evoke a faith response. We can believe and tell the story the three woman can no longer proclaim as living witnesses in history. In the written gospel Jesus becomes story. In the written gospel Mary Magdalene, Mary the mother of James and Joses, and Salome become midwives at the boundary of the written narrative, ready to help hearers' faith come to birth, expecting us to dialogue with their silence, to interpret this first of the written gospels.

The real ending of Mark's gospel is in the responses of its hearers and readers. The women's awe and ecstasy at the empty tomb and the news Jesus is risen create the threshold where faith begins in Jesus, the Christ, the Son of God. The written story is the catalyst for new generations coming to faith.

1 With what range of thoughts and feelings do you respond to the ending of Mark's gospel at 16.8 with its emphasis on the empty tomb and the women's ecstatic amazement? What do you prefer about the alternate endings that finish the gospel with appearances of Jesus risen?

2 How is the end of the gospel a beginning for you?

3 In Mark's gospel Jesus' women disciples Mary Magdalene, Mary the mother of James and Joses, and Salome witness his crucifixion and death, burial, and find his tomb empty. What authority do you give their witness?

4 Why do you think Mark's gospel only mentions Jesus' women disciples near its end? How do their credentials as disciples who have followed, served, and accompanied Jesus change the way you picture Jesus' public ministry in Galilee and his journey to Jerusalem?

5 Who in the gospel narrative most inspires you to follow Jesus? What is a scene in which you wish you had taken part?

6 What new questions has studying Mark's gospel raised for you?

7 To what actions does the Jesus of Mark's gospel call you today in our world?